DrawPlus X4
Resource Guide

This Resource Guide, and the software described in it, is furnished under an end user License Agreement, which is included with the product. The agreement specifies the permitted and prohibited uses.

Trademarks

DrawPlus is a registered trademark of Serif (Europe) Ltd.

All Serif product names are trademarks of Serif (Europe) Ltd.

Microsoft, Windows, and the Windows logo are registered trademarks of Microsoft Corporation. All other trademarks acknowledged.

Windows Vista and the Windows Vista Start button are trademarks or registered trademarks of Microsoft Corporation in the United States and/or other countries.

Adobe Flash is a registered trademark of Adobe Systems Incorporated in the United States and/or other countries.

Wacom, the logo and Intuos are trademarks or registered trademarks of the Wacom Company, Ltd.

Copyrights

TrueType font samples from Serif FontPacks © Serif (Europe) Ltd.

Digital Images © 2008 Hemera Technologies Inc. All Rights Reserved.

Digital Images © 2008 Jupiterimages Corporation, All Rights Reserved.

Digital Images © 2008 Jupiterimages France SAS, All Rights Reserved.

Bitstream Font content © 1981-2005 Bitstream Inc. All rights reserved.

The Sentry Spelling-Checker Engine © 2000 Wintertree Software Inc.

Panose Typeface Matching System © 1991, 1992, 1995-1997 Hewlett-Packard Corporation.

Portions graphics import/export technology © LEAD Technologies, Inc. & Eastman Kodak Company.

Anti-Grain Geometry - Version 2.4 © 2002-2005 Maxim Shemanarev (McSeem)

PANTONE® Colors displayed in the software application or in the user documentation may not match PANTONE-identified standards. Consult current PANTONE Color Publications for accurate color. PANTONE® and other Pantone, Inc. trademarks are the property of Pantone, Inc. © Pantone, Inc., 2005.

Pantone, Inc. is the copyright owner of color data and/or software which are licensed to Serif (Europe) Ltd. to distribute for use only in combination with DrawPlus. PANTONE Color Data and/or Software shall not be copied onto another disk or into memory unless as part of the execution of DrawPlus.

© 2010 Serif (Europe) Ltd. All rights reserved. No part of this Resource Guide may be reproduced in any form without the express written permission of Serif (Europe) Ltd.

Serif DrawPlus X4 © 2010 Serif (Europe) Ltd. All rights reserved.

Companies and names used in samples are fictitious.

How to contact us

Contacting Serif technical support

Our support mission is to provide fast, friendly technical advice and support from a team of on-call experts. Technical support is provided from our web support page, and useful information can be obtained via our web-based forums (see below). There are no pricing policies after the 30 day money back guarantee period.

UK/International/
US Technical Support: http://www.serif.com/support

Additional Serif contact information

Web:

Serif Website: http://www.serif.com

Forums: http://www.serif.com/forums.asp

Main office (UK, Europe):

The Software Centre, PO Box 2000, Nottingham, NG11 7GW, UK

Main: (0115) 914 2000

Registration (UK only):   (0800) 376 1989

Sales (UK only):   (0800) 376 7070

Customer Service
(UK/International):   http://www.serif.com/support

General Fax: (0115) 914 2020

North American office (US, Canada):

The Software Center, 13 Columbia Drive, Suite 5, Amherst NH 03031, USA

Main: (603) 889-8650

Registration: (800) 794-6876

Sales: (800) 55-SERIF or 557-3743

Customer Service: http://www.serif.com/support

General Fax: (603) 889-1127

International enquiries

Please contact our main office.

Introduction

Welcome to the DrawPlus X4 Resource Guide! Whether you are new to DrawPlus or an experienced user, this guide provides content to help you get the best out of the program.

Offering a range of beginner-level and advanced tutorials, along with full-colour previews of DrawPlus's design templates, samples, and gallery elements, we hope you'll find this guide to be a valuable resource that you'll return to time and time again.

The Resource Guide is organized into the following chapters:

1: Tutorials

Provides introductory exercises to help new users master the basics, and more challenging projects for experienced users.

2: Gallery

Provides thumbnail previews of the content provided on the **Gallery** tab.

3: Effects

Provides thumbnail previews of the preset effects that you can apply with a single click from the **Effects** tab.

4: Brushes

Showcases the categorized natural stroke and spray brushes provided on the **Brushes** tab.

5: Design Templates

A useful reference gallery showing all of the design templates included with DrawPlus X4.

6: Samples

A gallery of examples to illustrate the capabilities of DrawPlus.

Contents

Introduction

Chapter I - Tutorials

Chapter 2 - Gallery

Chapter 4 - Brushes   293

Chapter 5 - Design Templates   307

Chapter 6 - Samples   331

Tutorials

In this chapter, you'll find a selection of illustrated, step-by-step tutorials and projects, divided into the following categories:

Learning the Basics—If you're new to DrawPlus, we suggest you start with this section. These exercises allow you to experiment with basic creative tools and techniques. Topics such as lines, shapes, fills, brushes, and text are explored.

Projects—The projects reinforce the use of multiple tools and provide a problem/solution approach to creative design challenges. Fantastic stopframe and keyframe animation techniques are also covered!

Accessing the tutorials

You can access the tutorials in one of the following ways:

- From the Startup Wizard, under **View**, click **Browse Tutorials**.
- From DrawPlus, click **Help** and then click **Tutorials**.

Accessing the sample files

Throughout the tutorials, you'll be prompted to access sample files that are referred to in the tutorials. All samples are accessible via the Internet at the following location:

http://go.serif.com/resources/DPX4

If you've clicked on a file, you can either open or save the file. We recommend you save the file to your desktop or a named folder on your computer.

Learning the Basics

In this chapter, you'll find a selection of simple step-by-step exercises, which allow you to experiment with basic creative tools and techniques.

If you're new to DrawPlus, we suggest you start with these tutorials before moving on to the other tutorials.

Lines

⬚ ⬚ Being able to draw and edit lines is an essential technique to DrawPlus. In this tutorial, you'll learn how to use the **Pen** and **Node Tools** to best advantage.

By the end of this tutorial you will be able to:

- Import an image file.

- Adjust the transparency of an image.

- Trace around an object using the **Pen** tool.

- Adjust curves using nodes and control handles.

- Create a silhouette from an image.

> Mastering the **Pen** and **Node Tools** won't be an easy task, however, they are amongst the most useful tools that DrawPlus has to offer and will open up endless possibilities for your artwork.

Go to **http://go.serif.com/resources/DPX4** to download the following tutorial project file(s):

○ **bird.jpg**

Let's begin...

- In the Startup Wizard, choose **Drawing**, select a page size of your choice and click **OK**.

To import the photo:

1   On the Drawing toolbar, click  **Insert Picture**.

2   In the **Insert Picture** dialog, locate the **bird.jpg** file, click to select it and then click **Open.**

3   Click on your page to place the photo at actual size.

On the HintLine toolbar, click ⊕ **Zoom In** or drag the Zoom slider to zoom into the image.

4   We're now going to trace the outline. You can make this easier by reducing the opacity of the image. With the image selected, on the **Colour** tab, set the **Opacity slider** to **50%**.

To use the Pen Tool:

1   On the Drawing toolbar, click the 🖊 **Pen Tool**.

   At the left of the Pen context toolbar, notice that the 🖊 **Pen Tool** has two creation modes:

   - ⌒ **Smooth joins**

   - ⌃ **Sharp joins**

   These options let you create smooth curve or sharp 'cusp' points as you lay down the nodes that make up your curve. As our image is predominantly comprised of curves, we'll work in **Smooth joins** creation mode.

2   On the context toolbar, click ⌒ **Smooth joins**.

3   Click where the wing meets the head, then continue clicking to place 'nodes' around the outline. (You don't have to be exact; we'll tidy up later...)

   The following images show the order of the places we clicked to trace the outline of the bird in an anti-clockwise direction.

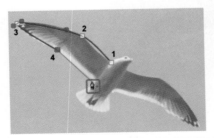

   Note that we used a 3pt red line for clarity and only placed nodes at key points where the line changed direction.

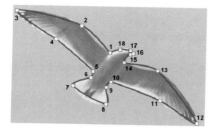

4   When you reach the last node (18 in our example), close the shape.

- On the Line context toolbar, click ⊬ **Close Curve**.
  - or -

- Hover over the last node and click when the cursor changes to ⊕○.

When you have completed your outline, like us, you will find that some areas of your curve need to be adjusted.

We'll do this next.

 Don't forget to save your work!

Adjusting lines with the Node Tool

There are several ways to edit lines, we'll only look at the ones we need for our shape. For more detail, see 'Editing lines and shapes' in online Help.

To adjust the line:

1   On the Drawing toolbar, click the ▷ **Node Tool**.

2   Click and drag on the first segment of the wing, so that it matches the curve of the photo.

3   Working anti-clockwise, drag the third section of wing into position.

4   As you work around the line, you'll notice that changing one section also alters the next.

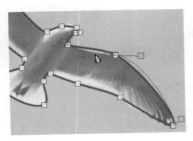

We can stop this happening by changing the **node type**.

Node types

Curves consist of curve segments, nodes and control handles. When you click on a node, the ⟋🖱∧∩∧ **node type** buttons become available for selection from the context toolbar. The behaviour of the control handles, and the curvature of the segments on either side of a node, depend on whether the node is sharp, smooth, symmetric, or smart.

(See 'Changing nodes and line segments' in the 'Editing lines and shapes' online Help topic.)

To change node type:

1   Click the ▷ **Node Tool**, select the object and then select the node you want to change (**Shift**-click to select multiple nodes).

2   On the context toolbar, click 🖱 **Sharp corner** to change the node type.

3   To shape the line to the wing, click and then drag the Bézier handle until the line follows the edge.

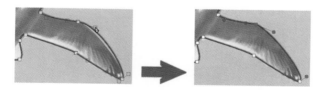

4   Repeat steps 2-3 to adjust any other lines.

 Don't forget to save your work!

To complete our design, on the **Swatch** tab, we changed the Line colour to black, and applied a black Fill to create a silhouette (see the **Fills I** tutorial).

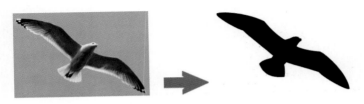

What you do with your outlined shapes is entirely up to you. Try modifying the colours, adding colour fills, or applying 3D effects to customize the objects. We'll leave you with a few examples that we used to customize a DrawPlus X4 sample.

Shapes 1

In this tutorial we are going to get creative with QuickShapes! DrawPlus has a lot of useful QuickShapes, and with a little imagination, they can be used to create a lot more than a few shapes on the page. Let's get started.

By the end of this tutorial you will be able to:

- Add QuickShapes to a page.

- Use the **Node** tool to edit Quickshapes.

Let's begin...

- In the Startup Wizard, choose **Drawing**, select a page size of your choice and click **OK**.

We'll begin by drawing a flower.

To draw a flower:

1   On the Drawing toolbar, click the **Pen Tool**.

2   Click once on the page to begin the line, and then, click and drag to create a short, curved line.

3   Press the **Esc** key to finish the line. You should now have a curved line with a start node and an end node.

4   With the line selected, on the **Line** tab, increase the line width to **10**pt.

5   On the Drawing toolbar, on the QuickShapes flyout, click the
     Quick Petal. Press and hold the **Shift** key while dragging on
    your page to draw the flower.

6   On the **Line** tab, change the line width to **1.5**pt and on the **Swatch**
    tab, click the **Fill** button and then click the white swatch to fill the
    shape white.

7   If necessary, re-position the flower head so it is at the top of the
    curved line. On the Drawing toolbar, click the  **Node Tool** and
    drag the leftmost node upwards until the petals just touch.

8   On the Drawing toolbar, in the QuickShapes flyout, click the **Quick Ellipse**. Press and hold the **Shift** key while dragging on your page to draw the centre of your flower. Re-position it as needed.

9   Now for the leaves. On the Drawing toolbar, in the QuickShapes flyout, click the **Quick Heart**. Drag on your page to draw the heart, and with the Node tool, drag the left node down to the bottom.

10   Finally, with the **Pointer Tool**, drag the leaves into position at the base of the stalk. We also rotated our leaves slightly to complete the effect.

That's it! You've drawn a flower using only a single line and a few QuickShapes.

Why not experiment with the **Quick Petal** nodes to see what other flower shapes you can create using the same techniques? (We'll look at adding colour in the **Fills 1** tutorial.)

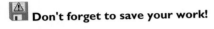 **Don't forget to save your work!**

That's it for part one! In **Shapes II** we'll get creative with a **Quick Ellipse** and show you what you can do with this and a few other basic QuickShapes.

Shapes II

In this tutorial we are going to draw several cartoons by using only basic QuickShapes! If you haven't done so already, you might find it easier to complete the **Shapes I** tutorial first.

By the end of this tutorial you will be able to:

- Create QuickShapes.

- Use **Convert to Curves** to create new shapes.

- Use the **Node** tool to transform shapes and lines.

- Copy shapes.

Let's begin...

If you look at the previous example, you'll notice that the cartoons all start from a basic pear shape. To create this, we will modify a Quick Ellipse using **Convert to Curves** and the **Node Tool**.

To draw a pear shape:

1   On the Drawing toolbar, on the QuickShapes flyout, click the
    ⊙ **Quick Ellipse** and drag on the page to create an ellipse.

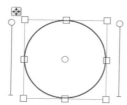

2   On the Drawing toolbar, click the ▷ **Node Tool**.

3   With the shape selected, on the **Arrange** tab, click ⊙ **Convert to Curves**. You'll see four 'nodes' appear on the ellipse's edge.

Converting a shape to curves allows you to edit it using the ▷ **Node Tool** and the **Curves context toolbar**.

4   Drag the topmost node upwards to create an egg shape.

5   Use the **Node** tool to add and move nodes, until your shape resembles a pear. For more information on editing lines, see the **Lines** tutorial.

Now we have the basic pear shape, let's take a brief look at how we can use it.

Example 1: Pear

To draw a pear:

1   Using the ![pointer] **Pointer Tool**, select the pear shape and copy it by holding the **Ctrl** key while dragging the shape. (Release the mouse button before the **Ctrl** key to complete the copy.)

2   On the Drawing toolbar, on the QuickShapes flyout, click the ![polygon] **Quick Polygon** and drag on the page to create a polygon.

3 Drag the topmost node to the left to reduce the number of sides to 3.

4 Using the **Pointer Tool**, drag the side handle inwards to make the shape thinner.

5 Hover next to a corner handle. When you see the ↻Rotate cursor, drag the object to rotate it.

6 Finally, drag the 'stalk' into position using the ✛ **Move** button. Congratulations! You've drawn a pear!

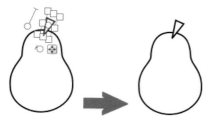

Hopefully you've now got the idea about how to copy, rotate and manipulate the nodes of QuickShapes. All of the following examples use our pear shape plus some other QuickShapes. We'll point these out in the 'shapes uses' section, but it's up to you to figure out how they go together!

 Don't forget to save your work!

Example 2: Penguin

The body of the penguin uses a copy of the pear shape. The wings, eyes and feet are basic QuickShapes:

- The wings are made from a single **Quick Polygon** which we copied and flipped using **Flip Horizontal** on the **Arrange** tab.

- The eyes are created from two **Quick Ellipses**. The 'pupil' is created by adjusting the nodes on the ellipse to create the shine. The right eye is a copy of the left.

Shapes used:

- 'Pear' (black)

- Quick Ellipse (red)

- Quick Polygon (blue)

> 💡 Save time and effort by copying elements that you have already created! You can always flip or rotate the copy if necessary.

 Don't forget to save your work!

Example 3: Rabbit

With the exception of the whiskers ( **Pen Tool**), the rabbit is also made out of three basic shapes. Again, where we had two elements that were basically the same, we saved time by copying and flipping the element using the **Arrange** tab.

Shapes used:

- 'Pear' (black)

- Quick Ellipse (red)

- Quick Polygon (blue)
  - and -

- Pen Tool (green lines)

You can re-arrange the **Z-order** of your objects using the tools— ⬚ **Bring to Front,** ⬚ **Forward One,** ⬚ **Back One** and ⬚ **Send to Back**—on the **Arrange** tab. See online Help for more information.

⚠ **Don't forget to save your work!**

Example 4: Horses

The horses might look complicated, but they still only use basic QuickShapes. The head is made from a resized copy of the original pear shape that has been flipped using **Flip Vertical** on the **Arrange** tab. The mane and tail are created using short lines drawn with the **Pencil Tool**.

Shapes used:

- 'Pear' (black)

- Quick Ellipse (red)

- Quick Polygon (blue)

- Quick Rectangle (purple)
  - and -

- Pencil Tool (green lines)

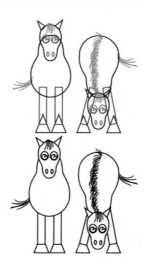

 Don't forget to save your work!

Now you've created your cartoons, let's add some colour in the **Fills I** tutorial.

Fills I

Building on the shapes created in the previous tutorials (**Shapes I** and **Shapes II**), we are now going to add a splash of colour.

By the end of this tutorial you will be able to:

- Change the colour of lines and fills using the **Swatch** and **Colour** tabs.

- Use the **Format Painter** to copy fill and line properties.

- Copy multiple objects.

Go to **http://go.serif.com/resources/DPX4** to download the following tutorial project file(s):

◉ **quickshapes.dpp**

Let's begin...

- In the Startup Wizard, choose **Open Saved Work**.

- Locate **QuickShapes.dpp** and click **Open**. Alternatively, if you
  have completed the previous tutorials, open the document
  containing the flower shapes.

Solid colour fills

To begin with we will look at applying solid colour fills to our shapes. For
this, we'll introduce the **Colour** and the **Swatch** tab. First, we are going
to add colour to a copy of our flower.

To copy objects:

1   With the ![pointer icon] **Pointer Tool**, click and drag to creating a selection
    around the flower. On release, the objects are selected.

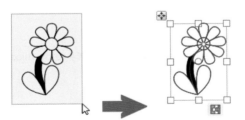

2   Hold the **Ctrl** key and drag the selected objects. (Release the mouse
button before the **Ctrl** key to complete the copy.) On release, the
new objects are selected.

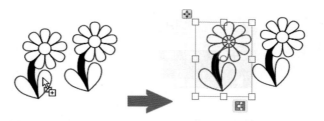

If the ▣ **Ungroup** button is displayed beneath any of your objects, click it to
ungroup the elements before you change the colour of the lines and fills.

To apply a solid fill and line colour (Swatch tab):

1   With the ▶ **Pointer Tool**, click to select the petals.

2　On the **Swatch** tab, the 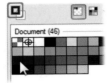 **Document Palette** is displayed.

- Click the **Line** button and then, click a dark blue swatch.

- Click the **Fill** button and then, click a lighter blue swatch.

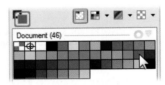

The flower petals are filled with the new colours.

3　Click to select the flower centre. Repeat step 2 to apply an orange outline and a yellow fill.

4   Click to select the flower stem. On the **Swatch** tab, click the arrow
on the 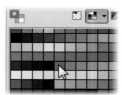 **Palettes** button and select **Standard RGB** from the
drop-down list. Click the **Line** button and then, click a dark green
swatch.

5   Finally, select the leaves. On the **Swatch** tab, apply a dark green line,
and a lighter green fill. (If you can't find a colour you like, try selecting
a different palette.)

Your flower is complete!

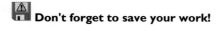

💡 Any colours that are used in your document are added to the 🔲 **Document
Palette** so that they are easy to find and reuse!

⚠️ **Don't forget to save your work!**

Next, we're going to look at copying formatting from one object to
another. We're going to use another flower for this.

To copy line and colour formatting:

1   Create another copy of the original flower.

2   With the ![pointer] **Pointer Tool**, click to select the coloured leaves, and then on the Standard toolbar, click ![icon] **Format Painter**.

3   Click on the black and white leaves of the copy. They update immediately.

4   Repeat this technique to colour the stem and centre of the flower.

The ![icon] **Format Painter** applies the colour and line properties (including weight, type, opacity, etc.) to an object. It doesn't affect the size of shape. Try it for yourself on some of the other shapes in the file! For more information about the **Format Painter**, see online Help.

To apply a solid fill and line colour (Colour tab):

1   With the **Pointer Tool**, click to select the back and white petals of the copy.

2   On the **Colour** tab the **HSL Colour Wheel** should be displayed. (If not, select it from the drop-down list.)

- Click the **Line** button and then, click in the triangle to select a colour saturation. To change the Hue, drag the small black circle in the outer wheel to a new location.

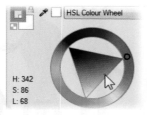

- Click the **Fill** button and then, repeat the process above to select a lighter fill colour.

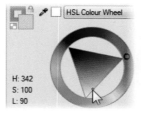

Your second flower is complete!

 Don't forget to save your work!

> When choosing line colours for cartoons, instead of using black, try a darker version of your fill colour. We think you'll be pleased with the results!

We used a combination of these three fill techniques to complete our cartoon animals. Why not give it a try yourself? In the final fill tutorial, **Fills II**, we'll look at gradient fills.

Fills II

In this tutorial, we are going to add gradient fills to some of the shapes created in the previous tutorials (**Shapes I** and **Shapes II**).

By the end of this tutorial you will be able to:

- Apply gradient fills from the **Swatch** tab.

- Apply gradient fills with the **Fill Tool**.

- Edit gradient fill colours.

- Use the **Fill Tool** to edit gradient fill paths.

- Save a gradient fill for later use.

Go to **http://go.serif.com/resources/DPX4** to download the following tutorial project file(s):

○ **quickshapes.dpp**

Let's begin...

- In the Startup Wizard, choose **Open Saved Work**.

- Locate **QuickShapes.dpp** and click **Open**. Alternatively, if you have completed the previous tutorials, open the document containing the flower shapes.

Gradient fills

Gradient fills can quickly add a lot more depth to your drawings by creating subtle shading. Once you know how to apply them, they are very quick, easy and effective to use. Although this tutorial concentrates on fills, gradient can be applied to lines in exactly the same way!

The following image shows a few different gradient fills that would suit our QuickShape flowers.

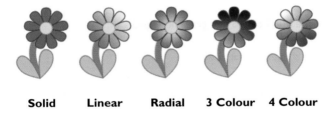

Solid   **Linear**   **Radial**   **3 Colour**   **4 Colour**

There are several ways to apply gradient fills, let's look at those now.

Create a copy first!

For this tutorial, each new gradient is going to be applied to a copy of the blue flower we created in **Fills I**.

To apply a gradient fill (Swatch tab):

1   Select the blue flower with the solid fill and create a new copy.

2   With the **Pointer Tool**, click to select the petals.

3   On the **Swatch** tab, click arrow on the **Gradient Palettes** button and select **Three Colour** from the drop-down list. Click the **Fill** button and then, click a blue gradient swatch to apply the gradient.

To apply a linear gradient fill (Fill Tool):

1   Select the blue flower with the solid fill and create a new copy.

2   With the **Pointer Tool**, click to select the petals.

3   On the Drawing toolbar, click the **Fill Tool**.

4   Drag from one side of the petals to the other to apply a linear gradient. By default, your current fill colour will be used as the start colour, and the end colour will be white.

Editing gradient fills with the Fill Tool

You can edit a gradient fill at any time. Clicking a new gradient swatch on
the **Swatch** tab will replace the current fill. To edit the current fill, you
need to use the **Fill Tool**.

To change a fill type:

1   Select the blue flower with the solid fill and create a new copy.

2   With the **Pointer Tool**, click to select the petals.

3   On the Drawing toolbar, click the **Fill Tool**.

4   On the Context toolbar, change the **Fill Style** to **Radial**. The fill is
    updated.

To change key colours (Context toolbar method):

1   With the petals selected, click the **Fill Tool**.

2   On the Context toolbar, select a new colour from the **Fill Start** drop-down list (we chose white).

3   Select a new colour from the **Fill End** drop-down list (we chose red). The fill is updated.

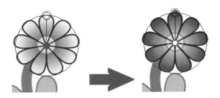

To change key colours (tab method):

1   With the petals selected, click the **Fill Tool**.

> Depending on the type of fill applied (linear, radial, ellipse, etc.), a fill path is displayed as one or more lines, with nodes marking where the spectrum between each key colour begins and ends.

2   Select a node with the ▷₊ node cursor, and then on the **Swatch** (or **Colour**) tab, click a new colour.
    - or -

Drag from a colour swatch on to any node to change the key colour of the node. The ⬚ cursor displays when you are over a node. Note that the node doesn't need to be selected.

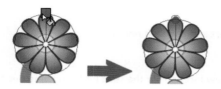

To add a key colour:

• Drag from a colour swatch on to a portion of the fill path where there is no node. The cursor changes to include a plus (+) sign ⬚ .

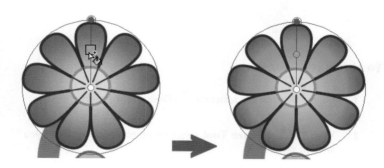

To delete a key colour:

• Select a colour node and press **Delete**.

To change the colour spread:

- Click and drag the fill path nodes.
  - or -

- Drag the start and end path nodes.
  - or -

- Click on a new location for the start node and drag out a new fill path.

To save a gradient fill:

1   On the **Swatch** tab, select the  **Document Palette**.

2   With the **Pointer Tool**, select the object containing the fill you want to save.

3   From the right-click menu, click **Add to Studio>Fill...**

4   In the dialog box, type a name for your fill and click **OK**.

Your fill is added to the **Document Palette**.

That's it! You should now be able to apply and edit gradient fills to any object. All it takes is a little practice.

To conclude this set of tutorials, here's an image created from only QuickShapes, the **Grass** spray brush, and the fill techniques that you have just learned. Why not try creating it yourself? Have fun!

Brushes I

The DrawPlus X4 **Brushes** tab includes a wide selection of pressure-sensitive, artistic brushes, which you can use to create some impressive effects. Many of the brushes are designed to allow you to create natural media strokes created by 'real' paintbrushes, pens, pencils, and other media. They are even applied in a similar way to the real thing!

In this tutorial, we'll introduce you to this exciting collection of drawing tools and show you how to use the brushes in your drawings.

By the end of this tutorial you will be able to:

- Use the **Brushes** tab, **Paintbrush Tool** and **Brush** context toolbar.

- Apply and edit brush strokes.

- Change brush stroke attributes.

A brush style can be applied to any type of line created in DrawPlus. We'll demonstrate a couple of techniques and illustrate how you can create different effects by adjusting brush stroke style and attributes.

We're going to work with the bunny drawing we created in an earlier tutorial (**Shapes II**). You can either create your own drawing or follow our tutorial exactly by working from our file.

Go to **http://go.serif.com/resources/DPX4** to download the following tutorial project file(s):

    ◉ **bunny.dpp**

Let's begin...

1   In the Startup Wizard, choose **Open Saved Work**.

2   Locate **bunny.dpp** and click **Open**.

At the moment, the bunny looks like a cartoon drawn with QuickShapes as it has smooth vector outlines.

There are two ways that we can give it a hand-drawn look:

- Convert the existing lines to brush strokes using the **Line** tab.

- Use the original lines as a guide (on Layer 1), and trace over them with the ✐ **Paintbrush Tool** (on another layer).

To convert lines to brush strokes:

1   With the  **Pointer Tool**, click and drag to create a selection around the bunny. On release, the objects are selected.

2   On the **Line** tab, click the ✏ **Brush Stroke** button. The default brush stroke is applied. Change the **Cap** style to ⊑ **Projecting Line Cap**.

3   Drag the slider to increase the line weight to **8pt**.

4   On the **Brushes** tab, in the drop-down brush category list, click **Draw**.

5   Finally, click the **Graphic Soft Outline 03** brush. Immediately, the bunny takes on a hand-drawn effect!

Zoom at 40%   Zoom at 200%

The Paintbrush tool

The **Paintbrush Tool** allows you to draw or paint with natural looking lines. DrawPlus includes ✒ 'stroke' and ☂ 'spray' brushes, stored on the **Brushes** tab. Here, brushes are divided into categories depending on their appearance. We'll be focussing on the ones in the **Draw** category.

> The **Paintbrush Tool** and the available brushes (and also the **Pencil Tool**) are pressure sensitive and will look very natural when used with either a pen and graphics tablet, or by using a combination of the mouse and **Pressure** tab (details are available in online Help).

> A pen and tablet works in a similar way to pencil and paper! With the pen, press and drag on the tablet to draw a line. Lift the pen to stop drawing. If you want a heavy, thick line, press hard on the tablet. For a thin, light line, use the pen lightly on the tablet. To select a line (or object, button etc.), hover the cursor over the line and then tap the pen on the tablet (this is the same as clicking with the left mouse button). You can also fine-tune any line using the **Pressure** tab. For the greatest control, don't forget to set up your tablet using the **Pressure Studio**. See online Help for details.

We'll look at this process now by tracing our bunny onto a new layer.

Zoom at 40%   Zoom at 200%

 To make the bunny easier to trace, we first selected all of objects on Layer 1 and, on the **Colour** tab, we reduced the line **Opacity** to **30%**.

To draw with the Paintbrush Tool:

1   On **Layers** tab, click ⊞ **Add Layer**. A new layer is added above Layer 1.

2   On the Hintline toolbar, use the Zoom buttons (or slider) to zoom into your drawing so that the bunny fills most of the workspace.

3   On the Drawing toolbar, click the 🖌 **Paintbrush Tool**.

4   On the **Brushes** tab, in the drop-down brush category list, click **Draw**.

5 Click the **Graphic Soft Outline 03** brush. This is a 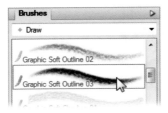 'stroke' bush, which is particularly good for drawing outlines.

6 On the Brush context toolbar, set the **Width** to **8pt**, and the **Smoothness** to **40%**.

7 On the **Line** tab, set the **Cap** to ⬒ **Projecting Line Cap** and the **Join** to ⬒ **Rounded Join**.

8 Use your pen and tablet (or mouse) to trace the first line by dragging on the page with the ✎ brush cursor.

9   Continue to trace around the outline of the bunny.

If you make a mistake on any of you lines (as we have done), you can quickly edit the path of the line with the  **Node Tool** (as we did in the **Lines** tutorial). Let's look at this briefly now.

To edit a brush line:

1   With the ✎ brush cursor, click to select the brush stroke that you want to edit.

2   To temporarily switch to the **Node Tool**, click and hold the **Ctrl** key.

3   Click and drag on the line and the control handles until the line is
correctly positioned.

Once you've completed your outline, you can also use the brushes to
shade, paint or 'colour-in' your drawing. The 🖌 'spray' brushes are great
for quickly filling in large blocks of colour, while the ✏ 'stroke' brushes
tend to work best for cross-hatching and more traditional shading
techniques.

To 'colour-in' with a brush:

1   On **Layers** tab, click ⊕ **Add Layer**. A new layer is added above
Layer 2. (We also hid Layer 1 by clicking ⊙.)

2   On the Hintline toolbar, use the Zoom buttons (or slider) to zoom
into your drawing so that the bunny fills most of the workspace.

3   On the Drawing toolbar, click the ✏ **Paintbrush Tool**.

4   On the **Brushes** tab, in the drop-down brush category list, click
Draw.

5   Click the **Chalk - Soft** brush. This is a 🖌 'spray' bush, which is particularly good for shading.

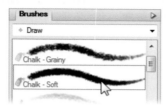

6   On the Brush context toolbar, set the **Width** to **6pt** and the **Smoothness** to around **20%**.

7   On the **Line** tab, set the **Cap** to ⊑ **Projecting Line Cap** and the **Join** to ⊔ **Rounded Join**.

8   Click and drag on the page, in the same way as you would shade in a drawing on paper, to shade in the pupil of the eye.

9   We can add some colour by simply changing the line colour on the **Colour** or **Swatch** tab. Here, we set the line to pink and coloured-in the nose.

10   Repeat the process, changing the brush type, colour and brush width
       until you have completely coloured-in your drawing. As we are
       working on a new layer, it doesn't matter if you go over the original
       lines, as we will fix that in a minute.

To re-colour a brush stroke:

1   Click to select the line.

2   On the **Swatch** (or **Colour**) tab, the **Line** button and then, select a
     new colour. The stroke is updated.

3   Finally, on the **Layers** tab, select layer 2 and click ◮ **Move Layer
     Up** to place it at the top of the stack. Your lines will now be on top
     of the coloured areas!

To finish our drawing, we applied a dark brown colour to our outline and
created a background using a soft smudge brush for the sky, and a realistic
grass brush from the brushes **Photo** category. (We also added some
whiskers and a carrot!) For more on brushes, why not try the **Brushes II**
tutorial? Don't forget that you'll also find much more detail on editing the
various settings in online Help.

Brushes II

As we've seen in the previous tutorial, **Brushes I**, the **Brushes** tab includes a wide selection of artistic brushes. Spray brushes in particular are great for filling in and shading large areas, just as an airbrush would be in the non-digital world. Many of the DrawPlus spray brushes create photo-realistic textures on the page.

In this tutorial, we'll focus on spray brushes to create an image similar to one found in the DrawPlus X4 Samples.

By the end of this tutorial you will be able to:

- Use layers to add depth to an image.

- Use spray brushes and change properties (colour and opacity).

- Create and edit spray brush strokes.

Go to **http://go.serif.com/resources/DPX4** to download the following tutorial project file(s):

🔘 **night.dpp**

Let's begin...

- In the Startup Wizard, choose **Open Saved Work**.

- Locate the **night.dpp** file and click **Open**.

Using the spray brushes

In the following sections, we'll use a selection of spray brushes to add clouds and trees to our starting image.

Spray brush types

On the **Brushes** tab, the spray brushes are denoted with the 🖌 icon. Spray brushes may be based on photo images or textures. Both can be recoloured.

To create our finished image, we're going to add various brush strokes to various layers within the document. We'll start by using a brush to add a few clouds.

To add the clouds:

1   On the **Layers** tab, click on the **Clouds I** layer to make it the active layer.

2   On the Drawing toolbar, click the 🖌 **Paintbrush Tool**.

3   On the **Brushes** tab, in the drop-down brush category list, click **Nature**.

4   Click the **Fog** brush.

5   On the **Swatch** tab, click the **Line** button and then, click a light grey swatch.

6   At the top of the workspace, on the Brush context toolbar, set the brush **Width** to **200pt** and the **Opacity** to **20%**.

7   Click and drag a zig-zag line down the page to paint a layer of cloud in the sky. The cloud appears behind the moon as it's on the layer below the **Moon** layer.

Next we'll add some cloud in front of the moon.

8   On the **Layers** tab, click on the **Clouds 2** layer to make it the active layer.

9   On the **Swatch** tab, set the line colour to the lightest grey swatch.

10   On the Brush context toolbar, set the brush **Width** to **124pt** and the **Opacity** to **100%**.

11   Click and drag across the page to paint some cloud across the moon.

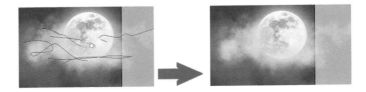

12   Continue building up the cloud until you've achieved the effect you want. Vary the opacity of different strokes can help make the cloud look more authentic.

To add the trees:

1   On the **Layers** tab, click on the **Trees 1** layer.

2   On the **Brushes** tab, in the **Nature** category, click the **Trees** brush.

3   On the Brush context toolbar, set the brush **Width** to **200pt** and the **Opacity** to **100%**.

4   Click and drag a free-flowing line in the lower section of your page to create the treetops.

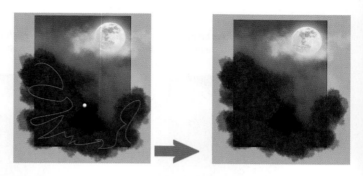

Next we'll add some foreground trees.

5   On the **Layers** tab, click on the **Trees 2** layer.

6   On the **Brushes** tab, in the **Nature** category, click the **Moss** brush.

7   On the Brush context toolbar, set the brush **Width** to **200pt** and the **Opacity** to **100%**.

8   Click and drag a free-flowing line in the lower section of your page to create the treetops.

9   Finally, on the **Layers** tab, click on the **Trees 3** layer.

10   On the **Swatch** tab, set the line colour to a yellow swatch.

11   With the **Moss** brush, paint a smaller line over the lower-left of the
     tree section. The photo brush colour is altered to have a yellow hue.

That's it! Your spray brush work is complete.

Optional step: Adding the silhouette

To complete our night image, we added a couple of bat silhouettes. We've
included the bat in the DrawPlus file, **silhouettes.dpp** for you to use.
Otherwise, why not create your own by following the steps in our **Lines**
tutorial?

 Go to **http://go.serif.com/resources/DPX4** to download the
following tutorial project file(s):

○ **silhouettes.dpp**

To add the silhouette:

1   On the **Layers** tab, click on the **Silhouette** layer to make it the
     active layer.

2   On the **File** menu, click **Open**.

3   Browse to your **silhouettes.dpp** file and click **Open**.

4   Right-click the silhouette you want to use in your image and click
     Copy. Close the silhouettes.dpp file.

5   Back in the **night.dpp** file, right-click on the page and click **Paste**.

6   Drag the pasted silhouette into position, resizing it as required.

> To create additional silhouettes, simply create copies. Don't forget that you can flip,
> rotate and resize the silhouettes.

If you've followed all of the steps in this tutorial, you should now have an
image that resembles ours.

We hope you've enjoyed working with the spray brushes. Remember, the best way to find out what each brush does is to experiment freely. Have fun!

We look forward to seeing your spray brush creations on the www.drawplus.com website!

Creating Brushes

DrawPlus includes a wide selection of pressure-sensitive brushes. However, if you can't find the perfect brush for your project, you can also create your own!

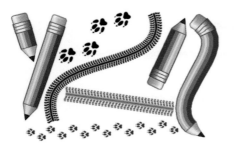

Stroke Brushes

Spray Brushes

By the end of this tutorial you will be able to:

- Create a new brush category.

- Create a non-repeating (stretching) stroke brush.

- Create a simple, repeating stroke brush.

- Create a spray brush.

- Copy and edit an existing brush.

Brush categories

DrawPlus includes 🖋 'stroke' and 🖌 'spray' brushes, stored on the **Brushes** tab. Here, brushes are divided into categories depending on their appearance.

To create a brush category:

1   On the **Brushes** tab, in the upper category drop-down list box, select **Global**.

2   Right-click on the category list box and click **Add...**

 If you right-click on an existing category, your custom category will be added as a 'subcategory' of the selected category.

3   In the dialog, type a name for your category, e.g., My Brushes, and click **OK**.

4   The category displays in the tab's drop-down list.

To rename a category:

•   Right-click a category and choose **Rename**.

To delete a category:

•   Right-click a category and choose **Delete**.

> ⚠ Do you really want to delete? Deleting categories and brushes will permanently remove them from the DrawPlus environment.

Brush textures

Before you start creating your brush, you need to choose the brush texture (design). A brush texture is simply a vector or bitmap file which is loaded for the brush type. There are several points to bear in mind:

File type and bit depth

- Any file format can be used, although we recommend using a 24 or 32 bit depth PNG with transparency for colour brushes.

- An 8 bit depth greyscale (no transparency) PNG in recommended for black and white brushes.

- If you aren't using an image with a transparent background, then your texture background should be pure white (RGB 255, 255, 255) as DrawPlus will create the transparency from this.

Shape/orientation

- **Stroke brushes**—For best results, the brush texture should be rectangular in shape with landscape orientation.

- **Spray brushes**—The design can be of any shape and any orientation, ideally contained within a square boundary.

- Crop as close as possible to the image so that there is very little or no white space around it.

Resolution

- **Stroke brushes**—This depends on the texture and repeat type, around 1500 pixels wide and 500 pixels high is good for most textures.

- **Spray brushes**—For best results, the resolution should be 512 pixels wide by 512 pixels high.

Creating stroke brushes

Stroke brushes have either a **Stretching** or **Repeating** body repeat method.

The following illustrations show how changing this setting affects the appearance of a brush stroke.

- **Stretching:** The 'body' of the brush is stretched along the length of the stroke.

- **Repeating:** A portion of the brush body is repeated over the length of the stroke.

    The number of times the portion is repeated is configurable and can range between one (**Simple**) and ten.

Now that you understand the basic principles, let's put them into practice. In the following section, we'll show you how to create:

- **a stretching bitmap photo brush**.

- **a simple one-part repeating bitmap texture brush**.

Stretching bitmap stroke brush

Assume now that we want to create a stroke brush based on an image of a pencil.

 Go to **http://go.serif.com/resources/DPX4** to download the following tutorial project file(s):

 pencil.png

You can create your brush textures from an exported drawing in DrawPlus as we have done for the pencil, or from a photo. Use Image Cutout Studio to remove the background and then export the image as a **24 or 32 bit depth PNG with transparency**. If you are creating a black and white brush, export the image as an **8 bit depth PNG without transparency**.

Let's begin...

- In the Startup Wizard, choose **Drawing**, select a page size of your choice and click **OK**.

To create a stretching bitmap stroke brush:

1   Open the **Brushes** tab, in the category drop-down list, select the **My Brushes** category we created earlier.

2   Right-click anywhere in the brushes list and click **Add Stroke...**

3   In the **Brush Edit** dialog, click **Browse for a different texture**. In the **Open** dialog, browse to the **pencil.png** (32 bit depth with transparency) file and click **Open**.

4   The **Brush Name** box is populated with the name of your texture file. (You can change it if desired.)

5   Select the category in which to store your brush.

6   In the **Body repeat method** drop-down list, select **None - (Stretch)**.

7   In the image preview window, note the vertical blue lines on either side of the image.

Creating Brushes

Click and drag these lines to define the **Head** and **Tail** (the sections you want to protect), and the **Body** (the section you want to stretch).

Note the updated values in the **Head**, **Body**, and **Tail** boxes.

8 Click **OK**.

9 Over on the **Brushes** tab, your new brush displays in the category you specified.

10 Make a few brush strokes to see what effects you can create... Why not try changing the line colour to see what happens?

One-part repeating bitmap texture brush

Let's now create a new stroke brush based on a repeating pattern. We are going to show you two examples, a paw print brush and a tyre tread.

Go to **http://go.serif.com/resources/DPX4** to download the following tutorial project file(s):

○ **paw.png**

○ **tread.png**

Example I

The paw image is an easy image to create a repeating brush from as it has a good repeating pattern with plenty of 'white' space in between the patterns. This makes it easy to create seamless joins.

To create a bitmap texture brush:

1   Open the **Brushes** tab, in the category drop-down list, select the **My Brushes** category we created earlier.

2   Right-click anywhere in the brushes list and click **Add Stroke...**

3   In the **Brush Edit** dialog, click **Browse for a different texture.** In the **Open** dialog, browse to the **paw.png** (8 bit depth no transparency) file and click **Open**.

4   The **Brush Name** box is populated with the name of your texture file. (You can change it if desired.)

5   Select the category in which to store your brush.

6   In the **Body repeat method** drop-down list, select **Simple**.

7 In the image preview window, note the vertical blue lines on either side of the image.

Click and drag these lines to define the **Head** and **Tail** (the sections you want to protect), and the **Body** (the section you want to repeat).

8 Click **OK**.

9 On the **Brushes** tab, your new brush displays in the category list you specified. Make a few strokes to try it out...

Example 2

All simple repeating brushes are created in this way. The trick is to ensure that your repeating section joins are seamless. To complete this section, we'll show you another simple repeating brush to give you an idea of how to create seamless joins on a more complex pattern.

1   Repeat steps 1-7 to create your **tread.png** (8 bit depth no transparency) texture brush.

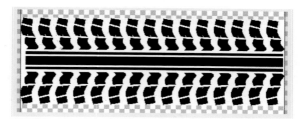

Click and drag these lines to define the **Head** and **Tail** (the sections you want to protect), and the **Body** (the section you want to repeat). Notice how we've lined up the **Body** section so that it will create a seamless repeat. (On some images, this may be a case of trial and error!)

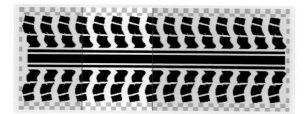

2   Click **OK**.

3 On the **Brushes** tab, your new brush displays in the category list you specified. Make a few strokes to try it out...

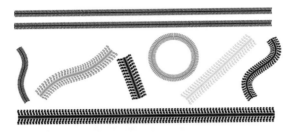

Creating spray brushes

Like stroke brushes, spray brushes can be based on any image type. The difference lies in the way they are created. Before you start creating your brush, you need to choose the texture (design) on which to base it. (See the **Brush textures** section for image guidelines.)

Let's now create a new spray brush based on several images.

Go to **http://go.serif.com/resources/DPX4** to download the following tutorial project file(s):

- bat1.png

- bat2.png

- bat3.png

- bat4.png

- bat5.png

To create a spray brush:

1   Open the **Brushes** tab, in the category drop-down list, select the **My Brushes** category we created earlier.

2   Right-click anywhere in the brushes list and click **Add Spray...**

3   In the **Spray Brush Edit** dialog, click the **Click to add a spray nozzle...** button. In the **Open** dialog, browse to the file you want to use (**bat1.png**) for your new brush. Double-click the file, or select it and click **Open**.

    The **Brush Name** box is populated with the name of your texture file. (You can change it if desired.)

4   In the **Category** drop-down list, select the category in which you
    want to save the brush.

5   (Optional) Repeat step 3 to add additional nozzles (**Bat2.png**,
    Bat3.png, **Bat4.png** and **Bat5.png**).

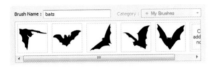

6   Adjust the settings described below to achieve the desired effect for
    your brush.

- **Texture Selection Controlle**r (multiple nozzles only):
  This setting changes the way in which the various nozzle
  textures are applied to the page.

  For example, select **Random** to randomly mix up the
  order of nozzle textures; select **Pressure** to change nozzle
  texture according to the pressure applied with the brush
  (via pen and tablet or the **Pressure** tab).

- **Position / Size Dynamics** settings: These settings change
  the positioning of the nozzle(s) as the brush is 'sprayed' on
  the page. (To create our bat brush, you'll need to increase
  the **Spacing** value to around 105%.) For detailed
  information on the settings, see online Help.

- **Rotation Dynamics** settings: These settings change the
  rotation of the nozzle(s) as the brush is sprayed on the
  page.

7   When you are happy with your brush design, click **OK** to save it to the **Brushes** tab.

8   Test out your new brush, varying the width of your strokes.

We also created a similar brush using full colour leaf images.

Go to **http://go.serif.com/resources/DPX4** to download the following tutorial project file(s):

○ **leaf1.png**

○ **leaf2.png**

○ **leaf3.png**

Remember, you can use as many overlapping lines as you need to when building up a texture!

Copying and editing brushes

At some point you'll want to make changes to an existing brush, or to a brush you've created yourself.

You can customize the predefined DrawPlus brushes. However, any changes you make will overwrite the existing brush presets so we suggest that you copy the brush to your own category before editing it (see "**Brush categories**" at the beginning of this tutorial).

 If you are certain that you want to edit and overwrite the brush, choose the **Edit** option. If you choose this method, you will not be able to save the brush type to a new category and your changes will **permanently modify** the original brush.

To copy and edit a brush:

1   On the **Brushes** tab, right-click the brush you want to edit and click **Copy**.

2   In the **Brush Edit** dialog, you can:

  • Rename the brush. (Note that DrawPlus gives it the default name "Copy of ...")

  • Save the brush in a different category.

  • Change the repeat areas and the body repeat method (stroke brushes).

  • Browse for a different brush texture or nozzle (spray brushes).

  • Adjust texture selection controller, position dynamics, and rotation dynamics settings (spray brushes).

3   Make the desired changes and then click **OK** to save your edited brush.

You can customize brush strokes directly using the Brush context toolbar—click the **Brush** option to open the **Stroke/Spray Brush Edit** dialogs. Any changes you make in this way will only affect the selected brush stroke and will not modify the brush stored in the gallery.

We've covered a lot of material in this tutorial—you've learned how to create a variety of different brushes, and how to copy and edit existing brushes.

We've introduced you to the basic procedures, but encourage you to get creative and try creating your own set of custom brushes.

We've introduced you to the basic procedures, but encourage you to get creative and try creating your own set of custom brushes.

And just in case you want to have a go at creating our cheerful caterpillar brush, we've provided the file for you!

 Go to **http://go.serif.com/resources/DPX4** to download the following tutorial project file(s):

   ◉ **caterpillar.png**

Text

DrawPlus offers three types of text to use in your projects, frame text, shape text and artistic text.

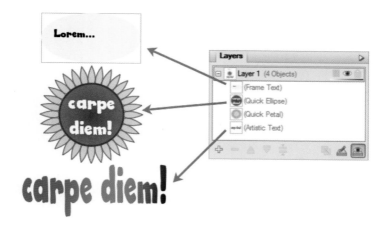

You can use the same methods to perform operations such as selecting, editing, and formatting all types of text. For detailed information, visit the online Help.

By the end of this tutorial you will be able to:

- Work with artistic, frame and shape text.

- Create, edit, and format all types of text.

- Create text-on-a-path.

- Change the shape and fill of text frames.

In this tutorial, we'll add some text to a greetings card. You can either create a card from scratch using one of the folded publications templates (available from the **Start New Drawing** option on the Startup Wizard), or you can work with the card that we have already partially designed.

 Go to **http://go.serif.com/resources/DPX4** to download the
following tutorial project file(s):

⊙ **card.dpp**

Let's begin...

- In the Startup Wizard, choose **Open Saved Work**.

- Locate the **poster.dpp** file and click **Open**.

The card opens with Page 1 displayed in the workspace.

Let's start by adding some artistic text!

To create artistic text:

1   On the Drawing toolbar, click the ![A] **Artistic Text** tool.

2   Click on the page to create an insertion point.

3   On the Text context toolbar, in the **Font** drop-down list, select **Apple Boy BTN** and sent the size to **72pt**.

4   On the **Swatch** tab, select the **Fill** button and click a black swatch.

5   Type your greeting.

Next, we'll use the properties of artistic text to make it a little more exciting!

To resize and rotate artistic text:

1   With the  **Pointer Tool**, click on the top-centre handle of the text box and drag upwards. Notice that this stretches the text.

2   Next, click right-centre handle of the text box and drag inwards. Notice that this squashes the text.

3   To rotate the text, hover next to a corner handle. When you see the ↖ cursor, click and drag to rotate the object.

4   Finally, click and drag the **Move** button to position the text.

Why not add some colour to your text? With the text box selected, go to the **Swatch** tab. Click the **Fill** button and then expand the **Gradient Fills** flyout. Then select a category and click one of the swatches to apply a gradient fill.

For more on using fills, make sure you visit the tutorials **Fills I** and **Fills II**.

Now that we've completed the front of our card, let's move on to the back. Here, we'll show you how to fit text to a curve. In the **Pages** tab, click to select page 3.

Now let's create a new artistic text object...

To create artistic text (alternative method):

1   On the Drawing toolbar, click the **A** **Artistic Text** tool.

2   Click and drag on the page to set the font size to approximately **25pt**.

3   Type a card slogan (we used our website address).

If you're not happy with the way the default font looks, you can easily change it. We'll do this next.

This method of formatting applies to all types of text.

To select and format existing text:

1   On the Drawing toolbar, click the 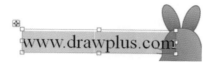 **Artistic Text** tool.

2   Click inside the text box next to the first letter, and then drag to highlight all of the text. (You can also press **Ctrl + A** or triple click.) The selected text is highlighted blue.

3   On the Text context toolbar, in the **Font** drop-down list, select **Apple Boy BTN**.

4   On the **Swatch** tab, select the **Fill** button and click a green swatch. The text formatting is updated.

Next, we'll fit our text to a curved path.

To put text on a path:

1   With the text object still selected, on the Text context toolbar, expand the 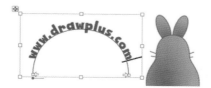 **Preset Text Paths** flyout and click to apply the **Curved Text - Top Circle** preset.

2   To adjust the path, hold the **Ctrl** key, and with the **Node Tool**, click the green start node and drag upwards.

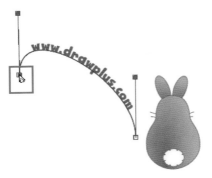

3   (Optional) To adjust the slope of the path, hold the **Ctrl** key, and with the **Node Tool**, drag the curve handle.

4   Finally, to change where the text starts, ensure that the Artistic Text tool is selected and click in the text to create an insertion point.

5   Drag the Start point arrow to the right to push the text towards the end of the curve.

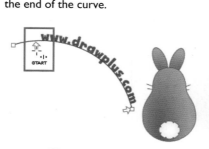

6   Finally, to place the text beneath the curve line, drag the alignment node to the bottom of the bar.

7   That's it, your curved text is complete! If you've followed the steps exactly, the text should resemble our illustration.

You can also fit text to any curve, shape or line that is drawn on the page. For more information, see 'Fitting text to a path' in online Help.

Now let's make the inside of our card a little more interesting. In the **Pages** tab, click to select page 2. On the inside pages of our card, we have a sunflower created from a Quick Petal and a Quick Ellipse.

Let's add our greeting to the inside of the flower (i.e. the Quick Ellipse).

To create shape text:

1   On the Drawing toolbar, click the A **Artistic Text** tool and then click on the Quick Ellipse. An insertion point begins to flash in the centre of the shape.

2   On the **Swatch** tab, click the **Fill** button, and click the white swatch.

3   On the Text context toolbar, select the **Apple Boy BTN** font and set the font size to 36pt. (You might need to adjust this to suit your message.)

4 Type the greeting you used on the front of the card.

Congratulations! You've just created shape text! We'll finish the card by creating a text frame.

To create a text frame:

1 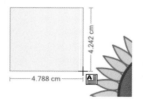 On the Drawing toolbar, on the Text Frames flyout, click the **Frame Text** tool.

2 In the upper-left corner of the card, click and drag to create a small text frame.

3 On the Text context toolbar, select the **Apple Boy BTN** font and set the size to **24pt**.

4 On the **Swatch** tab, click the **Fill** button, and click the black swatch.

5 Type 'To... '.

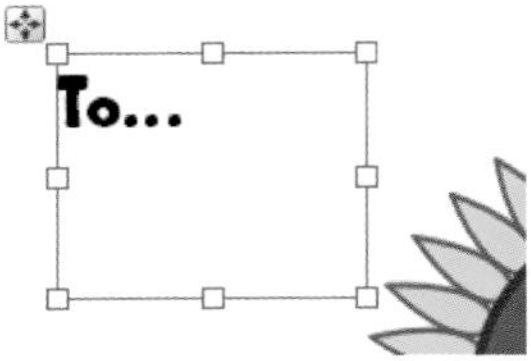

You have created a basic text frame. However, we don't have to stick with a basic rectangle. Let's get creative!

(Optional) To adjust the shape, line and fill of a text frame:

1 With the **Pointer Tool** click to select the text frame.

2 On the **Line** tab, increase the line width to around **2pt**.

3 On the **Swatch** tab, apply a light fill and a black line.

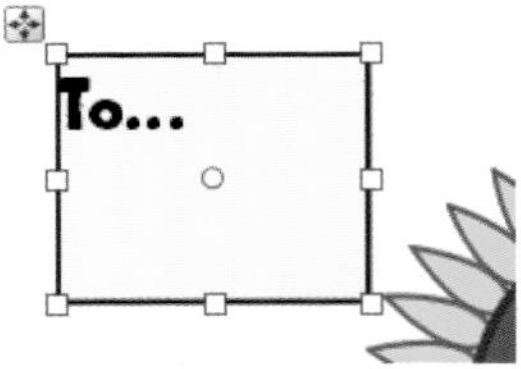

4   On the Drawing toolbar, click the **Node Tool** and on the Context toolbar, choose **Quick Thought** from the Shaped frame drop-down menu. Adjust the direction of the bubbles by dragging the bottom node left or right.

5   Finally, with the **Pointer Tool**, resize the frame so that it fits all of your text. Notice that, unlike before, when you resize the frame, the text properties do not change as this is Frame Text.

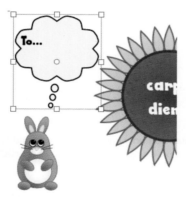

6 Repeat steps 2-5 to create a "From" text frame. Why not try a different shape and line style?

Although a shaped text frame and shape text can look similar on the page, they are treated differently by DrawPlus. If you look at the layers tab, text frames and artistic text always appear as text. However, shape text only appears as its containing shape. This is because text frames have very different behaviour. To find out more about adjusting text flow and linking text frames, see online Help.

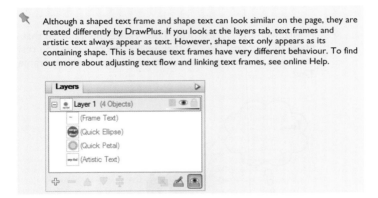

That's it, your card is complete! You now know how to edit and format text, apply text effects, create text-on-a-path, and create new artistic, shape and frame text objects.

The skills you have acquired should be sufficient for most of your DrawPlus projects!

Projects

These projects reinforce the use of multiple tools and provide a problem/solution approach to creative design challenges.

We'll also look at the two forms of animation in DrawPlus—Keyframe and Stopframe animation.

Wax Seal

In this tutorial, we'll show you how to create a 'wax seal' effect. You'll use some basic QuickShapes and the **Freeform Paint Tool**, then apply filter effects to add depth and dimension to your shapes.

Once you've created your basic wax seal, you can get creative and adapt it for a multitude of purposes.

By the end of this tutorial you will be able to:

- Create constrained QuickShapes.

- Use the **Freeform Paint Tool**.

- Use the **Colour** and **Line** tabs to apply properties to a shape.

- Use the **Filter Effects** dialog to apply bevel and emboss effects.

Let's begin...

- In the Startup Wizard, choose **Drawing**, select a page size of your choice and click **OK**.

To create the basic shape:

1   On the Drawing toolbar, on the ▢⁻ QuickShapes flyout, click the ◯ **Quick Ellipse**, then hold down the **Shift** key and draw a circle about 10cm in diameter.

    Let's now add a red fill to our circle.

2   On the **Colour** tab, click the **Fill** button, then, click a point in the red section of the colour wheel.

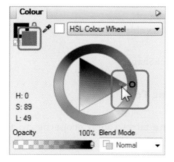

3   On the **Line** tab, remove the outline from your shape by clicking ▢ **None**.

4   On the Drawing toolbar, click the ✐ **Freeform Paint Tool** and on the context toolbar, select the ◯ **Round Nib** and increase the width to **30pt**.

5   Click and drag at various points around your circle to create an
     uneven border.

6   Increase the brush width to **60pt** and then click and drag to add a
     few larger circular shapes to the border.

     You can vary the brush width, and the click and drag/click process as
     much as you want to achieve the desired effect.

To combine shapes:

1   With the 🖰 **Pointer Tool**, click and drag to creating a selection
     around the objects. On release, the objects are selected.

2   On the **Arrange** tab, click **Add** to combine all of the shapes into one. Don't worry if your shape doesn't look exactly like our illustration—no two wax 'blobs' are alike!

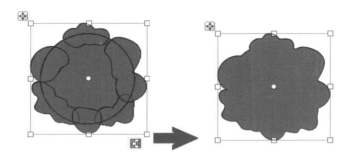

Don't forget to save your work!

Now we have the shape, we'll add the waxy finish using the **Filter Effects**.

To add filter effects:

1   With the **Pointer Tool**, click to select the shape.

2   On the Drawing toolbar, click **Filter Effects**.

3   In the **Filter Effects** dialog, in the **Effects** list, click to select **Bevel and Emboss**.

4   In the **Bevel and Emboss** section, set the **Style** to **Inner Bevel**.
     Drag the **Blur** slider to the right to increase the bevel effect (about
     25 works well). The object will preview on the page (or in the dialog
     if the ▷ preview window is open). We also increased the **Depth**
     slider to about 125.

5   Click **OK**.

⚠ **Don't forget to save your work!**

Creating the seal

You can create anything you want, from a simple letter, to a more intricate combination of shapes and letters.

To create the centre ring:

1   On the [icon] QuickShapes flyout, click the [icon] **Quick Ellipse**, then hold down the **Shift** key and draw a circle inside your wax blob. Apply the same fill you used before and remove the outline.

2   On the Drawing toolbar, click [icon] **Filter Effects**.

3   In the **Filter Effects** dialog, select **Bevel and Emboss** and this time, simply increase the **Depth** to around **200** and leave the other settings at their default. Click **OK**.

4   With the [icon] **Pointer Tool**, click to select the circle and press **Ctrl+C** to copy it, followed by **Ctrl+V** to paste. The copied object is placed on top of the previous circle.

5 Press and hold **Ctrl** and **Shift** while resizing the top circle to make it smaller.

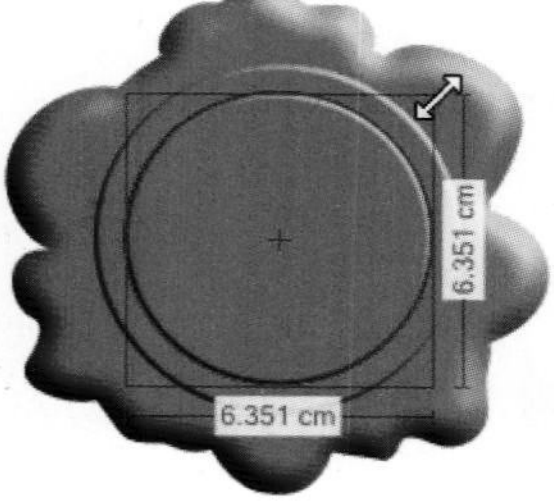

Holding the **Shift** key when resizing constrains the aspect ratio of an object. Holding the **Ctrl** key while resizing ensures that the centre position remains the same.

6 On the Drawing toolbar, click *fx* **Filter Effects**. This time, change the Bevel and Emboss **Style** to **Outer Bevel**. Change the **Angle** to **230**. Click **OK**.

We'll complete the design by using a single letter, x.

To create the design:

1   On the Drawing toolbar, click the $\boxed{A}$ **Artistic Text** button.

2   Click and drag on the page to set the size of the font to approximately **160pt**.

3   Type the letter 'X' and use the ⊞ **Move** button to position the text in the centre of the inner ring.

4   With the $\boxed{\nwarrow}$ **Pointer Tool**, click to select the text object and on the **Colour** tab, set the **Fill** to the same colour as you've used throughout.

5   On the Drawing toolbar, click *fx* **Filter Effects**. In the **Filter Effects** dialog, add an **Inner Bevel** with the following settings: **Blur:** 2; **Depth:** 150; **Angle:** 230.

     Congratulations, you've created your first wax seal!

⚠️ **Don't forget to save your work!**

As you can see, the entire process mainly consists of creating and manipulating QuickShapes and text objects, and then applying bevel and emboss effects to them.

Once you've mastered these techniques, you can create any design you want. Below are a couple of examples to get you started.

Torn Paper

In this tutorial, you will combine DrawPlus tools and techniques to make a variety of torn paper effects— including a pirate's treasure map.

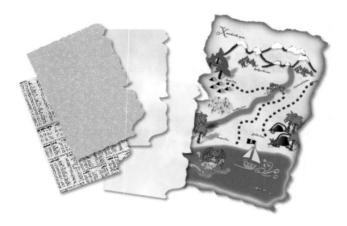

By the end of this tutorial you will be able to:

- Draw lines and shapes with the **Pencil Tool**.

- Combine shapes using the **Subtract** command.

- Apply bitmap and gradient fills.

- Apply a drop shadow with the **Shadow Tool**.

- Use the **Roughen Tool** to turn smooth edges into jagged outlines.

- Apply paper textures.

Let's begin...

- In the Startup Wizard, choose **Drawing**, select a page size of your choice and click **OK**.

To create the shape

1   On the Drawing toolbar, on the QuickShapes flyout, click the 🔲 **Quick Rectangle** and draw a rectangle to represent your piece of paper.

2   On the Drawing toolbar, click the ✏️ **Pencil Tool** and draw a jagged line to represent the torn edge of the paper.

Continue the line outside the edge of the rectangle and connect the start and end nodes to create a shape.

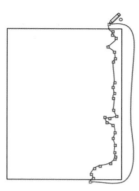

When you release the mouse button, your new shape will sit on top of the rectangle, hiding its edge.

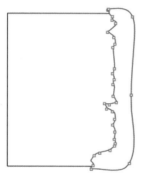

3   On the **Edit** menu, choose **Select All** (or press **Ctrl + A**) to select both the rectangle and the freehand shape.

4   On the **Arrange** tab, click the   **Subtract** button. DrawPlus removes the section of the rectangle that is overlapped by the freehand shape.

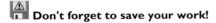 **Don't forget to save your work!**

Now that we've got the basic outline for our piece of torn paper, there are a multitude of things we can do with it. We'll show you a few examples then we'll let you experiment on your own...

Adding a bitmap fill

To achieve this effect we applied one of DrawPlus's predefined bitmap fills to the shape, and then added a drop shadow.

To apply a bitmap fill

1   With the ▶ **Pointer Tool**, click the shape to select it.

2   On the **Swatch** tab, click the arrow on ▦▾ **Bitmap** button and select **Misc** from the drop-down list.

3   Click the **Misc06** swatch to apply it to your shape.

4   On the **Line** tab, click  **None** to remove the shape's outline.

To create a drop shadow

1   With the **Pointer Tool**, click the shape to select it.

2   On the Drawing Toolbar, click the **Shadow Tool**.

3   Click and drag down and slightly right to apply the shadow.

Creating a marbled effect

Simple but effective, this marbled effect was created by applying and editing a plasma fill.

We also removed the outline and applied a drop shadow.

To apply and edit a plasma fill

1   With the 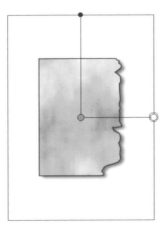 **Pointer Tool**, click the shape to select it.

2   On the **Swatch** tab, click the arrow on the [image] **Gradient** button and select **Plasma** from the drop-down list.

3   Apply any gradient fill by clicking its swatch.

4   With the shape still selected, on the Drawing toolbar, click the [image] **Fill** tool. The shape's fill path and nodes display.

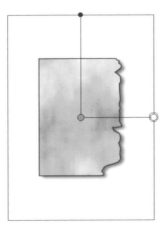

5   On the **Swatch** tab, click the arrow on the [image] **Palettes** button and select a palette from the drop-down list.

6   Drag colour swatches from the tab to the fill path to change and add key colours.

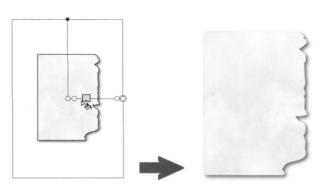

Creating a rough edge

The simplest method of all—we quickly roughened the edge of this piece of paper using the **Roughen** tool.

1   With the ▶ **Pointer Tool**, click the shape to select it.

2   On the Drawing toolbar, click the ✴ **Roughen Tool**.

3   Click and drag either upwards or downwards. The further you drag, the more pronounced the effect. On release, the effect is applied.

Only the outline of the shape is affected and there's no internal distortion—so if you have applied a bitmap fill, for example, the fill remains intact.

- To remove a roughen effect from an object, double-click it with the **Roughen** tool, or click **Remove Roughen Effect** on the context toolbar.

Adding texture

DrawPlus provides you with a number of other fills and textures that are particularly suitable for creating paper effects.

Create a paper texture on the layer:

- Click ■ **Apply Paper Texture**, then choose from the wide selection of textures available in the **Bitmap Selector** dialog.

Create a paper texture on the object:

1 Create an exact copy of your paper object and paste it on top of the existing object.

2 On the **Swatch** tab, click the arrow on ⊞▾ **Bitmap** button and select **Paper Textures** from the drop-down list. Try the various fills until you find a texture you like.

3 On the **Colour** tab, set the **Blend Mode** to **Screen**. The colour of the object beneath is revealed with the texture on top.

As you can see, once you have created the basic template for your torn paper, there are many things you can do with it. This tutorial has illustrated a few ideas, but we hope it has also inspired you to explore some of your own. We'll leave you with a final example.

Example: Treasure map

Here we created a treasure map using a variety of DrawPlus tools and features. We'll explain how we did it; however, rather than replicating our example exactly, you should have fun with this and explore your own ideas!

 Go to **http://go.serif.com/resources/DPX4** to download the following tutorial project file(s):

🌐 **map.dpp**

 The individual elements of the treasure map are on **Layer 2**—you'll need to make **Layer 2** visible and hide the other layers.

Burnt edge effect

[fx] We wanted the edges of our map to look charred. To accomplish this, in the **Filter Effects** dialog, we added an **Inner Glow** using the following settings:

- **Blend Mode**: Multiply

- **Opacity**: 75

- **Blur**: 40.5pt

- **Intensity**: 15

- **Colour**: Mid brown—RGB(128, 80, 47)

Trees

We drew our two trees with the **Pencil Tool**, connecting the start and end nodes to make a closed shape. Each tree is made up of two shapes with a line and colour fill. The shapes were then **grouped** and the shadow applied with the **Shadow Tool**. The various groups of trees are simply copies, resized as necessary.

Caves

For the cave entrances, we used the **Pencil Tool**, connecting the start and end nodes to make a closed shape. We then applied a gradient fill to the shapes.

Tents

We used the **Straight Line Tool**, connecting the start and end nodes to make a closed shape. Each shape was given a solid colour fill. The campsite was made up of copies of this first tent.

Flowers

We made these with simple **Quick Petals**. The stems were drawn with the **Straight Line Tool**, and the leaves are **Quick Ellipses**.

Pirate Ship

A combination of shapes, lines, and fills was used to create our pirate ship with the **Pencil Tool**.

Fish

We used the **Pencil Tool** for the body, and a **Quick Ellipse** for the eye.

Mountains

We used the **Pencil Tool** to draw the mountain range. The snowy peaks were created as separate objects. We applied a drop shadow filter effect to each element to create a 3D effect.

River and paths

These were drawn with the **Pen Tool**. The river is a simple curved line, with a weight of 7.5pt. We applied drop shadow and feather filter effects to soften the edges. For the footpaths, we simply changed the line style to a dotted line on the **Line** tab.

Dragon

Our friendly dragon was created with the **Pencil Tool**, closing the shapes and applying fills where needed.

Gel Button

In this tutorial we'll create this impressive looking gel button in just a few easy steps.

By the end of this tutorial you will be able to:

- Create and manipulate QuickShapes.

- Use the **Colour** and **Line** tabs to apply properties to a shape.

- Work with gradient transparency.

- Use the **Filter Effects** dialog to apply feather effects.

- Group and ungroup objects.

Go to **http://go.serif.com/resources/DPX4** to download the following tutorial project file(s):

○ **gel.dpp**

Let's begin...

- In the Startup Wizard, choose **Drawing**, select a page size of your choice and click **OK**.

To create the basic shape:

1 On the left Drawing toolbar, on the QuickShapes flyout, click the  **Quick Rectangle**, then click and drag to draw a large rectangle on your page.

2 On the **Colour** tab, click the **Fill** button, and then apply a fill colour by clicking a point in the colour wheel. For optimum effect, choose an intense colour .

3 On the **Line** tab, remove the outline from your shape by selecting **None** from the line style drop-down list.

4 Drag the left sliding node all the way up to the top to round the corners fully.

5   Click the  **Pointer Tool**, then right-click the shape and choose **Copy**. Right-click again and choose **Paste**.

The new shape is pasted on top of the original and is selected by default.

6   On the **Colour** tab, apply a slightly lighter fill colour . (We used **H 144**, **S 56**, **L 47**.)

7   On the Drawing toolbar, click *fx* **Filter Effects**. In the **Filter Effects** dialog, select the **Feather** check box and set the **Blur** value to **10**. Click **OK**.

To create the glow:

1   Copy and paste this new shape and apply an even lighter colour fill (we used **H 144**, **S 79**, **L 51**). Open the **Filter Effects** dialog again and increase the **Blur** value to **14**.

2   With the new rectangle selected, click its upper size handle and drag down to make a thinner shape.

We now have our 'glowing' gel button, but we still need to add a reflection highlight.

To create the highlight:

1   Select the original shape and then copy and paste it. Now apply a
    white fill. This new shape will completely cover the three previous
    layers. In order to create our reflection effect, we need to edit this
    white shape using the **Node Tool**. To do this, we must first
    convert the object to curves.

Did you know that you can use the **Layers** tab to select objects? Each object has a
preview icon that gets larger when you hover over it. With the 🔲 **Auto Select**
button on, when you select an object on the page, it will also be highlighted in the
Layers tab.

2   With the white shape selected, on the **Arrange** tab, click
    ⟳ **Convert to Curves**.

3   Click the **Node Tool** and draw a selection bounding box around
    the two nodes at the lower edge of the shape. Click on one of the
    nodes and drag it up slightly—the other node will also move.

4 Repeat the previous step to move the upper two nodes.

5 Now click the **Pointer Tool**, select the white shape, and reduce its size slightly. Position the shape in the upper centre area of the button.

Our button looks very effective already. However, with another couple of steps we can make it look even more realistic. We want to soften the highlight slightly, at the lower edge only. We'll use a gradient transparency to achieve this effect.

6 With the reflection selected, on the Drawing toolbar, click the **Transparency Tool** and draw a transparency path from just above to just below the shape.

Transparency effects are great for highlights, shading and shadows, and simulating 'rendered' realism. All objects in DrawPlus have an overall **Opacity**. By default this is set to 100% (fully opaque). To make an object more transparent, drag the Opacity slider on the **Colour** tab towards 0% (fully transparent).

The **Transparency Tool** is used to create transparency gradients on an object

Congratulations, you've created your gel button. Now to add a shadow. This is an important step because it gives the button a translucent appearance.

To create the shadow:

1   Click the **Pointer Tool** and select the original large shape from your button—the easiest way is to select the object on the **Layers** tab. Copy and paste the shape and move it away from the button.

2   On the Drawing toolbar, click *fx* **Filter Effects**. Select the **Feather** check box and set the **Blur** value to **13**.

3   Copy and paste this new shape, make it smaller and lighter in colour .

4   Select both objects and on the **Align** tab, ensure that the **Include Page** option is cleared and then click **Centre Vertically** and **Centre Horizontally**. Finally click **Group** to group the objects together.

5   Now select your grouped shadow objects and on the **Arrange** tab click **Send to Back**. Adjust the size of the shadow if needed.

6   Finally, with the shadow still selected, on the **Colour** tab adjust the
    Opacity of the shadow to **45%**.

That's all there is to it! We hope you'll agree that the process of creating
this gel button is actually a fairly simple one, but the results are very
effective. Why not try creating other buttons using different colours?

Wine Glass

In this tutorial, we'll create a wine glass you can place on any background to show its transparency. This tutorial assumes that you are familiar with the main drawing and editing tools in DrawPlus. To help you with this more advanced project, we've created sample objects for you included in the resource file supplied with this tutorial.

By the end of this tutorial you will be able to:

- Apply simple fills and transparencies using the **Swatch** and **Transparency** tabs.

- Use the **Transparency Tool** to adjust the transparency of an object.

- Turn a basic line drawing into a realistic 3D image.

Go to **http://go.serif.com/resources/DPX4** to download the following tutorial project file(s):

glass.dpp

Let's begin...

- In the Startup Wizard, choose **Open Saved Work**.

- Locate the **glass.dpp** file and click **Open**.

> The first page of the document shows a **keyline** (line drawing) of the wine glass, and the last page the finished article. In between pages are labelled in stages.
>
> To navigate between pages, click the 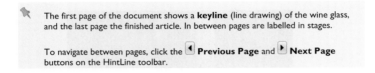 **Previous Page** and ▶ **Next Page** buttons on the HintLine toolbar.

Getting started:

1   Save the file under a new name. You will want to use the original project as a reference throughout the tutorial.

2   On the HintLine toolbar, click the ⬚ **Page Manager** and delete pages 2 to 7.

Save your changes.

3   Reopen the original file and keep it available for reference while you're working on the new file (use the **Window > Tile** command or adjust the windows for convenience).

Creating the Bowl

For this tutorial we'll remove any elements that aren't required, and bring it all together at the end. We'll begin with the top of the glass and work our way down. Since the wine glass is in keyline form to start with, you will only be able to select an element by clicking on the line itself.

To create the basic bowl:

1   In the **Layers** tab, select the 'Keyline' layer. Click the keyline of the 'bowl'.

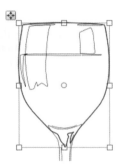

- On the **Colour** tab, apply a black fill and a set the **Opacity slider** to 10% opacity.

- Remove the keyline (outline)—on the **Line** tab select 🔲 **None**.

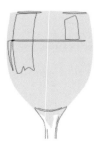

2   Select the left 'strip glow' and colour it solid white. Remove the keyline.

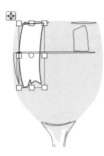

3   On the **Transparency** tab, in the **Gradient** drop-down list, select **Radial** and apply a radial transparency (we used **Radial 21**). Use the 🏆 **Transparency Tool** to adjust the transparency so its path looks like our illustration (**A/1**).

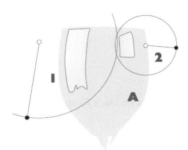

4   Repeat step 2 and 3 for the smaller strip glow (**A/2**).

📌   See glass.dpp, Stage 1 (Page 2) for the completed steps.

5   Copy the longer strip glow and paste it over itself—this trick gives a
sharper transparency. Do the same with the small strip glow, but
after pasting it, nudge it slightly down and to the left. This will give the
glass depth, as if light is also reflecting from the inside.

See glass.dpp, Stage 2 (Page 3)

6   Select the main bowl, copy and paste it, then give it a white fill
and increase the opacity to **20%**—it will be nearly invisible but
that's the effect we want. Make it slightly smaller by pressing **Ctrl**
while dragging inward on a corner handle.

7 The bowl shape should now sit in front of the other bowl, leaving a slightly darker edge. This should give a glass a believable outline. In the following illustration, we've given the shape a false outline to illustrate its position.

Next, we'll use this new bowl to enhance the glass effect by creating various transparency effects. Each time, we'll create a copy of the bowl object we create and use the copy as the basis for the following step.

 Don't forget to save your work!

To enhance the glass effect:

1   With the new bowl object selected, apply the **Ellipse 19** transparency.

2   Click the ☒ **Transparency Tool** and drag the centre transparency node to position the transparency outside the object's right edge, slightly overlapping it to create a feathered soft edge.

In the overlap zone, you should see a blending into white where less transparency reveals the new bowl's white colour. We'll duplicate this object and adjust the transparency on each copy to extend the feathered edge.

3   Copy and paste the new bowl, then drag its transparency zone up and adjust the nodes so that it resembles our screenshot.

4 Copy and paste again, and this time, adjust transparency so that it covers the upper portion of the bowl.

Now you'll see a consistent white blend that follows the side of the glass (this will become more obvious on a darker background). We'll use the same 'bowl' to add transparency in a couple of other areas.

5 Copy and paste again. This time we will create a white keyline for the inner bowl.

- remove the fill colour—on the **Swatch** tab, click to select the **Fill** swatch and then click the **None** swatch.

- apply a solid white line—on the **Line** tab, click the **Line** button and set the line thickness to **1pt**. Then, on the **Swatch** tab, click to select the **Line** swatch and set the colour to white.

- set the opacity to **100%**—on the **Colour** tab. drag the **Opacity slider** to the far right.

6   Drag the transparency (not the object!) up to the top left area, as
     shown in **D2**, and reshape it slightly to produce a light-reflective
     keyline that adds definition.

7   Copy and paste the newest bowl (with the amended keyline), and
     nudge the copy over to the right. Enlarge the transparency gradient,
     and position it to the right as we have done to create a stronger line
     down the side of the glass.

Don't forget to save your work!

The next few operations are more of the same, in that we're adding a few more reflective transparencies—but these will be small 'flares' around the rim, front, side, and base of the glass.

To add the bowl accents:

1   In the **Layers** tab, select the 'Accents' layer.

2   With the ![pointer tool icon] **Pointer Tool**, select the accent objects on bowl.

3   Remove the line and apply a white fill.

4   Apply an elliptical transparency from the ![transparency tool icon] **Transparency Tool** context toolbar and make adjustments as required so that the transparencies resemble our illustration (we've given each gradient a different colour to help you see what's going on).

5   Finally select the single line just above the stem and change the line
    colour to white. Apply an elliptical transparency and modify it so that
    it resembles our illustration. This will define the base of the bowl.

Against a coloured background, you should now have something
closely resembling our illustration!

 See glass.dpp, Stage 3 (Page 4). To display the background, simply make the
'background' layer visible.

 Don't forget to save your work!

Creating the Stem

Now we'll follow similar procedures for the base and stem. The approach is to apply a light base colour and then side highlights, followed by the flares to add realism. We'll concentrate more on speed than detail, to avoid repetition. Don't forget to remove keylines unless otherwise stated.

To create the stem:

1   On the **Layers** tab, hide the 'Accents' layer. Select the 'Keyline' layer and then select the keyline that defines the stem. Apply a black fill and solid 10% opacity. Copy and paste it in place, fill the copy with white, and add a 1pt white line.

2   Using our illustration as a guide, apply an elliptical transparency to the object and move the transparency (not the object) to the right of the stem, with a slight overlap.

3   Copy the object and paste it again, so it retains its white fill and line, then rotate and extend the transparency to resemble our illustration. This will give the base of the stem a reflective glow.

See glass.dpp, Stage 4 (Page 5).

Don't forget to save your work!

To finish off we'll apply the flares to the stem.

To add the stem accents:

1   On the **Layers** tab, make the 'Accents' layer visible and ensure that it is selected.

2   With the ⬉ **Pointer Tool**, **Shift**-click to select each of the accent lines and change the colour to white and increase the line width to 1pt.

3   Apply either a radial or elliptical transparency to each line using the ⬚ **Transparency Tool** context toolbar.
    Try to match the examples in the illustration below (we've given each gradient a different colour to help you see what's going on).

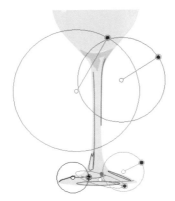

4   With the  **Pointer Tool**, **Shift**-click to select the remaining three shapes. Remove the line and apply a white fill. Reduce the **Opacity** to **40%**.

5   Apply either a radial or elliptical transparency to each line using the  **Transparency Tool** context toolbar. Try to match the examples in the illustration below (we've given each gradient a different colour to help you see what's going on).

See glass.dpp, Stage 5 (Page 6). To display the background, simply make the 'background' layer visible.

Don't forget to save your work!

Congratulations! Your glass is complete. All you need to do is add a coloured background to complete the effect. To do this, we created a layer called 'background' and then added a QuickShape that covered the whole page. We applied a gradient fill to the QuickShape and... voila!

Now that you've mastered this technique, why not try applying the same methods to other objects like glass buttons for your website; or use the skills you've learned to create shiny metallic objects and water effects.

Introducing Animation

DrawPlus X4 provides exciting functionality that lets you create and export Adobe® Flash™-based animations using keyframes. Combine this with the extensive drawing capabilities of DrawPlus, and you have all the tools you need to create impressive movies, cartoons, Web banners, and so on.

Introduction

The term **stopframe** (or **stop motion**) animation describes the conventional animation technique that makes static objects appear to move. The object is moved by very small amounts in successive frames, giving the impression of movement when the film is played.

In **keyframe** animation, a particular event or sequence of events is recreated in a series of snapshot images. The event is 'captured' at key moments (keyframes) where an object begins or ends an action. Animation between these keyframes is then calculated by the software—in this case, DrawPlus.

For example, suppose you want to create an animation of a bouncing ball. As the animator, you specify the start, end, and key intermediary positions of the ball, then DrawPlus smoothly fills in the gaps (a process known as **tweening**). At any point, you can fine-tune the animation to improve the duration, speed, and dynamics of the movement by adding or adjusting keyframes.

In the tutorials in this section, we will create both types of animation. In fact, within DrawPlus you can convert drawings (.dpp files) into both stopframe and keyframe animations, or you can take a stopframe animation file and use it to create a keyframe animation.

We'll now tell you a little bit more about how to go about creating an animation from scratch. However, if you want to just get stuck in, we'll see you again in the next tutorial, **Stopframe Animation**!

1: Storyboarding

A storyboard is a visual script of the shots and scene changes in a video or film—a plan that you can refer to as you work on your project.

The storyboarding process helps you to think about how you want your finished animation to look, how the story should unfold, and how best to convey your story to your audience.

Think about what you actually want to achieve, and then create a rough illustration of what will happen during the animation. You don't have to be an artist—rough sketches and stick figures will do just as well.

2: Starting the project and drawing the character

The way you create you character is quite personal. Some designers prefer to sketch their rough ideas with pencil and paper first, while others prefer to work directly with the DrawPlus drawing tools. We suggest you experiment with both techniques to see which you prefer.

- If you're sketching with DrawPlus tools, we recommend you use **QuickShapes** for drawing simple shapes, the 📝 **Pencil Tool** for drawing freeform lines and shapes, and the 🖊 **Pen Tool** for precise lines.

- You can fine-tune any line or curve by switching to the ▷ **Node Tool** and then adjusting the nodes and curves.

- If you have a drawing on paper that you'd like to use as the basis for your animation, scan it into your computer, save it as a graphics file, and then clean it up in DrawPlus. For information about importing scanned images, see online Help.

- If you're using a pen and tablet but are not too sure of your freehand drawing ability, you can place a printed image on the tablet and trace around its outlines.

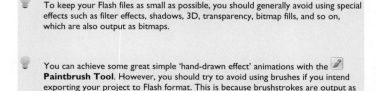

💡 To keep your Flash files as small as possible, you should generally avoid using special effects such as filter effects, shadows, 3D, transparency, bitmap fills, and so on, which are also output as bitmaps.

💡 You can achieve some great simple 'hand-drawn effect' animations with the 📝 **Paintbrush Tool**. However, you should try to avoid using brushes if you intend exporting your project to Flash format. This is because brushstrokes are output as bitmaps and will result in a large file size.

3: Cleaning up your sketch

When you have created your rough sketch, the next task is to clean up the outlines and shapes. During this stage, you also want to identify and isolate the components that will be moving independently—if you do this, you'll find it easier to adjust and manipulate these parts as you work on your animation keyframes later.

These components will vary depending on your character and story, and will range from the obvious—for example, body, legs, head—to the not so obvious (eyebrows, ears, hair, lips, and so on). Don't go into too much detail at first though. Often, the simpler characters are the most effective, and you can always add more detail later if necessary.

The following tips will help you to achieve the best results:

- If you're working from a scanned image, place your original sketch on Layer 1, add a new layer and then work on this layer as you carefully trace over the original lines. When you've finished, hide the layer containing the original sketch to check your results.

- Use **QuickShapes** for simple shapes.

- When using the 🖊 **Pencil Tool**, increase the **Smoothness** on the context toolbar. This reduces the number of nodes on the line, resulting in a 'clean,' smooth running animation.

- **Group** your items - You'll be able to move and rotate all the objects in the group at the same time. You'll find this useful when you are animating the project.

- If you need to rotate a component or group of components that are 'hinged' from a fixed point—a leg, arm, or head for example—you'll achieve a more realistic effect if you move the centre of rotation to the hinge point.

To do this, select the object or group and then click and drag the **rotation origin** to the desired position. You can then rotate the object from a corner selection handle. The illustration below shows how we could use this technique to rotate the head of our cartoon dog.

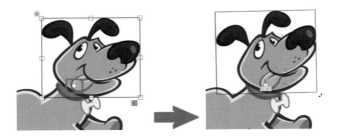

When drawing your character:

- Keep it simple and use clean lines and shapes. You can create a detailed version first, to get a good feel for your character, but before you start animating it, you'll need to simplify it. The simpler your character is, the easier it will be to animate.

- Keep your colours simple and in blocks rather than random lines. This will make it easier for you to blend the moving elements of your drawing, and will also help minimize your final file size.

- Use shadows to 'ground' and add depth to your animation. Without shadows, your characters will appear to float.

- If your character is going to talk, you'll need to draw variations of the mouth for different 'sounds.' If you don't require too much detail, you can get by with a few basic mouth shapes—A, E, I, O, U, F, M, P, S, TH, and so on. You'll also need some transition shapes to take you from one mouth form to the next.

- You may need to move small body parts individually at times, but you'll save yourself a lot of effort by creating groups of parts that you can move and rotate together.

4: Animating the character

When you are happy with your character, you're ready to animate it. Our running dog example uses only 3 keyframes, but complicated animations may have many more. Keyframes (and stopframes) are displayed as frames in the storyboard tab.

🔽 Go to **http://go.serif.com/resources/DPX4** to download the following tutorial project file(s):

    ◉ **dog.dpa**

When you ▶️▾ **Preview** your animation, you'll see that the dog runs at a constant speed as the animation loops.

5: Adding a background

You may not need or want a background for your animation. It all depends on your subject matter and the final effect you want to achieve. In some cases, a background will reduce the impact of the scene.

A background will provide 'context' for your character, but can also be useful for adding perspective and depth to a scene. There are several ways to do this, for example:

- Use strong (saturated) colours for your character and foreground, and less strong (unsaturated) colours for background objects.

- Make foreground elements sharp and clear and your background elements blurred.

Backgrounds don't have to be detailed. In this racehorse storyboard, the
roughly-sketched background gives the impression of motion and speed.

That's all there is to it! Now you know the principles, the next step is to
start animating... Good luck!

Stopframe Animation

Turn a cartoon into an animation using the traditional stopframe animation technique.

By the end of this tutorial you will be able to:

- Clone animation frames.

- Create a basic animation by manipulating elements.

- Export to an animated GIF file.

- Adjust animation export settings.

We have created a Stopframe animation file that contains a single frame with the fish drawing for you to animate.

Go to **http://go.serif.com/resources/DPX4** to download the following tutorial project file(s):

⊙ **cartoon.dpa**

Let's begin...

- In the Startup Wizard, choose **Open Saved Work**.

- Locate the **cartoon.dpa** file and click **Open**. The first frame of the animation is displayed in the workspace.

Animating the cartoon

Now we are going to animate the fish. This requires us to copy and change individual frames to create the animation. Don't worry, you won't need to draw anything! Instead, we are going to use DrawPlus to clone our animation for us.

To clone a frame:

1   At the bottom of the workspace, you'll see Frame I displayed in the **Frames** tab.

If you can't see the **Frames** tab, click the ⟶ **Open/Close** tab button at the bottom of the workspace.

2   On the **Frames** tab, click ⊞ **Clone Frame** DrawPlus creates an exact copy of the first frame and opens it in the workspace.

Next, we need to animate the fish. We are going to use a technique called **Onion Skinning** to view our frame-by-frame changes.

To animate frame 2:

1   On the Drawing toolbar, click the ![pointer] **Pointer Tool**. Click and drag
    to select the fish and the bubbles.

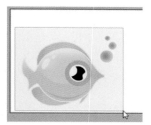

2   Press the right arrow key 10 times to move the fish to the right.

3   Click the ![onion] **Onion Skinning** button. Notice that you can now see
    the first frame beneath the current frame. This allows us to check
    how much each element has moved.

Now let's animate the fish. In each frame, we are going to make some
minor adjustments to the following:

●   The upper fin

●   The lower fin

●   The bubbles

4   Select the upper fin and drag it downwards slightly so that more of it is hidden by the body. Hide part of the lower fin in the same way.

5   Select the bubbles and drag them upwards. Finally, select the smallest bubble, press the **Ctrl** key and drag downwards to create a copy. Position this new bubble nearest the fish's mouth.

Click the  **Onion Skinning** button again to turn onion skinning off to ensure that you are happy with your frame.

Don't forget to save your work!

To create additional frames:

- Clone the most recent frame after making the adjustments.

- Select all of the elements and move them to the right with the arrow key. Move the elements by the same amount to create smooth movement.

- Animate the fins and the bubbles as in the previous steps, adding extra bubbles where necessary.

- Repeat the procedure until the fish reaches the other side of the screen (we used 12 frames).

- **Optional:** When your fish reaches the other side of the screen, select all of the elements and click ⚠ **Flip Horizontal** on the **Arrange** tab.

- Repeat the clone and move process to get your fish to swim back across the screen.

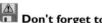 **Don't forget to save your work!**

To preview the animation:

- On the **Frames** tab, click 🖼 **Preview**.

- Click **Close** to exit the preview.

Our fish is swimming a little too quickly. We can change this by making each frame last a little longer. This is done by editing the frame properties.

To change the frame properties:

1   On the **Frames** tab, click  **Properties**.

2   In the **Animation Properties** dialog, increase the frame display time to 150 milliseconds (ms) and click **OK**.

All of the frames are updated.

To export the animation:

1   On the **Frames** tab, click **Export**.

2   In the **Export Optimizer** dialog, accept the default settings for **Animated GIF** and click **Export**.

3   In the **Export** dialog, type a name for your animation, choose a save location and click **Save**.

That's it! You can now view your creation by double-clicking to open it. Why not try animating some of your own DrawPlus creations?

Keyframe Animation

In this tutorial, we are going to create a fish tank complete with some swimming fish. Along the way, you'll learn about the special properties of keyframe animation, and how it can be used to animate objects without you having to draw every single frame.

By the end of this tutorial you will be able to:

- Insert a movie clip.

- Manipulate an object's motion path.

- Use the AutoRun feature to automatically update object creation and placement as you work.

- Use an object envelope to modify an object's rate of change over time.

- Use a mask to hide unwanted areas.

- Export to .swf format.

- Go to **http://go.serif.com/resources/DPX4** to download the following tutorial project file(s):

  ○ **tank.dpa**

Let's begin...

- In the Startup Wizard, choose **Open Saved Work**.

- Locate **tank.dpa** and click **Open**. The first frame of the animation is displayed in the workspace.

In the first frame of the animation, we've created a background that will serve as our fish tank. Of course, you can't have a fish tank without fish, so let's add some! We've created the fish for you, but you could always use your own...

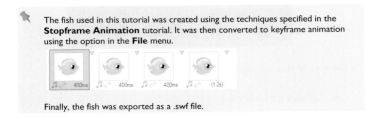

The fish used in this tutorial was created using the techniques specified in the **Stopframe Animation** tutorial. It was then converted to keyframe animation using the option in the **File** menu.

Finally, the fish was exported as a .swf file.

Go to **http://go.serif.com/resources/DPX4** to download the following tutorial project file(s):

○ **fish.swf**

To insert a movie clip:

1 We want to add our movie clip to a new layer. On the **Layers** tab, click ⊞ **Add Layer**.

2 Click the new layer to select it.

3 Go to **Insert > Movie Clip...**

4 Locate **fish.swf** and click **Open**.

5   Position the $\overset{+}{\triangleright}$ cursor on the grey workspace, just outside the
    top of the page and click once to place the movie clip at its
    default size. The clip displays the first frame.

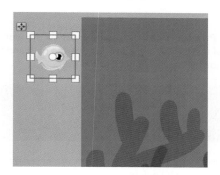

If we now preview the animation, the fish won't appear as it is not placed
on the main page. We can use this to our advantage when making the fish
'swim' across the tank from one side to the other. We can do this by
adding keyframes.

To add keyframes:

1   On the **Storyboard** tab, click 🖼 **Insert**.

2   In the **Insert Keyframes** dialog, in the **Number of
    keyframes** box, enter **9**. Click **OK**.

    The inserted keyframes are displayed in the **Storyboard** tab.

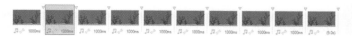

Click on any of the frames in the **Storyboard** tab. Notice that they are
exact copies of the first frame you created. This makes it much easier to
animate the objects. Let's now make the fish swim across the tank.

To animate the fish:

1   On the **Storyboard** tab, click to select the last frame in the sequence.

2   With the  **Pointer Tool**, drag the fish clip to the workspace on the right of the tank background. Notice the path and light-grey nodes showing the movement of the fish?

These represent the position of the automatically generated **motion tween** at each keyframe.

3   On the **Storyboard** tab, click to select the fifth frame in the sequence. Notice how the fish jumps to the corresponding node as it follows the motion tween.

4   To preview your animation, on the **Storyboard** tab, in the **Preview** drop-down list, click **Preview in Flash Player**. You should now see the fish swimming at a constant speed in a straight line across the tank.

Now that our fish is swimming across the tank, we can edit each keyframe to make the fish swim in a more interesting pattern. Let's do this now.

To edit keyframes:

1   On the **Storyboard** tab, click to select the fifth frame in the sequence.

2   With the ↖ **Pointer Tool**, drag the fish clip down towards the bottom of the tank. Notice how the path and nodes update in the other keyframes.

3   Click ▶▾ **Preview** to preview the animation.

4   On the **Storyboard** tab, click to select the seventh frame in the sequence. The node representing keyframe 5 has turned dark grey. This is because it is now a **key object**—in other words, you have defined that the fish must be in that position on that frame. Tweened objects are automatically generated by DrawPlus.

5   With the ↖ **Pointer Tool**, drag the fish clip upwards slightly. Notice that the path between frames 1 and 5 does not change as it is set between two key objects.

6   Click **Preview** to preview the animation. You should see
your fish swimming across the screen following the path you
specified.

When you preview your animation, you'll see that the fish moves at a
constant speed throughout the entire animation. This may be the effect
you require, but suppose you want to vary the speed of an object as it
moves through a scene? Read on!

Adjusting object envelopes

When you select an object that is part of a 'run sequence' (such as the
bone in our animation), the **Easing** tab becomes available.

In DrawPlus keyframe animations, the **Easing** tab provides a drop-down list of **envelopes** (Position, Morph, Scale, Rotation, Skew, Colour, and Transparency). These envelopes work in similar ways to control how an object's properties change over time, from keyframe to keyframe. Once you learn how to display and modify one type of envelope, you can apply the same principle to the others.

By default, DrawPlus applies a constant rate of change to all envelopes, but you can adjust this by modifying the envelope profile settings.

In this section, we'll make the fish appear to accelerate as it swims through the tank by applying and modifying a **position envelope**.

To apply a position envelope:

1   Open keyframe 1 and select the fish clip.

2   On the **Easing** tab, expand the Envelopes drop-down list and select the **Position Envelope**.

    Below the drop-down list, in the Envelope Profile pane, the blue diagonal line represents the rate of change of the fish's position from this keyframe to the next.

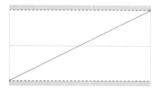

    By default, the rate of change is constant, but we can change this by adjusting the gradient of the profile.

3   Click a point in the middle of the blue line and drag it up towards the top of the pane.

4   Notice that the nodes on the downward curve start off quite far apart and then get closer together.

5   Preview your animation again. You should see the fish swim into the tank quickly and then slow up as it reaches the bottom of the curve (where the nodes get closer together) and then, swim off at a constant speed.

To stop our fish from being lonely, let's add another!

To insert a clip using AutoRun:

1   Click the ⏩▾ **AutoRun** button to enable this feature. By default, any new objects you create or reposition on any keyframe will now automatically run to the end of the storyboard.

2   Select keyframe 1 and then, go to **Insert > Movie Clip...**

3   Locate **fish.swf** and click **Open**.

4   Position the ⌖ cursor on the grey workspace on the opposite
     side to the first fish click once to place the movie clip at its
     default size.

If you now take a look at your storyboard, you'll see that
DrawPlus has placed a copy of the fish in all subsequent
keyframes.

5   On the Standard toolbar, click ◮ **Flip Horizontal**.

6   On the toolbar beneath the clip, click the ⮫ **Update attributes
     forwards** button. In the dialog, ensure **To end of storyboard**
     is displayed and click **OK**. Your second fish will now be facing
     left throughout the animation.

7   Click the ⏩▾ **AutoRun** button to disable this feature. Now
     you're ready to animate the path of the fish as you did with the
     first example!

Masking unwanted areas

If you're happy with your animation, you're almost ready to export it. However, because our animation goes outside the page, if it was resized, you'd see the fish swimming outside the tank.

We can easily fix this by adding a **mask**.

To add a mask:

1   On the **Layers** tab, click  **Add Layer**. Rename the new layer 'Mask'.

2   Select the first frame. Working on the **Mask** layer, click the **Quick Rectangle** and draw a rectangle that covers the page. On the **Swatch** tab, apply a bright colour to the fill and outline.

    This rectangle shape will act as a 'window'.

3   On the **Transform** tab, set the exact dimensions to 854 pix wide by 480 pix high.

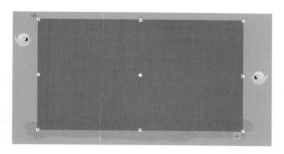

4   ⬚ ⬚ On the **Align** tab, click **Centre Horizontally** and **Centre Vertically**.

5   On the toolbar beneath the rectangle, click ▷▷ **Run placement forwards**. In the dialog, ensure **To end of storyboard** is displayed and click **OK**. Your rectangle will now appear throughout the animation.

6   On the **Layers** tab, right-click the **Mask** layer and click **Layer Properties...** In the **Layer Properties** dialog, in the **Attributes** section:

   •   Select the **Locked** check box.

   •   Select the **Mask** check box and then in the drop-down layers list, select **2**.

       This tells DrawPlus that we want this layer to mask both layers. (If we'd chosen to mask 1 layer, the mask would not hide objects on the **background** layer.)

- Click **OK**.

7   On the **Layers** tab, the ⓜ **Mask** and 🔒 **Locked** icons now
    display next to the **Mask** layer. The colour of the layers also
    change to clearly show the mask layer and the layer being
    masked.

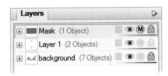

Until you lock a mask layer, the mask object, and the objects outside of the mask
area will show on the page. As soon as the layer is locked, it becomes transparent
and all objects outside of the mask are hidden from view.

8   As soon as the mask is locked, only the objects within the mask
    area can be seen—if you open frame 1, you'll see that the fish
    appear to have disappeared. Don't worry, they are only hidden
    as you can see by clicking through each frame.

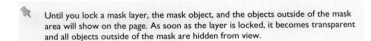

9   Preview your animation and resize the window to see the mask
    in action!

Exporting your animation

You can export to the following formats:

- Adobe Shockwave Flash file (.swf)

- Video (choose from .mov, .stv, .avi, .wmf file formats)

- Screensaver (.scr)

- Flash Lite/ i-Mode (a lightweight version of .swf, optimized for viewing on mobile phones and other devices)

- Image (a wide range of formats are supported, see online Help for details)

For this project, we will export our animation to a standard Shockwave Flash .swf file.

To export to Adobe Shockwave Flash:

1   On the **File** menu, point to **Export** and then click **Export as Flash SWF**..

2   Choose a file name and save location for your .swf file and then click **Save**.

3   The **Keyframe Animation Export** dialog displays the progress of the export and closes when export is complete.

    Simply browse to locate the file and then double-click to open it.

We hope that you have enjoyed working through this project and are happy with the resulting animation. Don't forget, you can add as many fish as you want! We hope that you are now comfortable with the basics of keyframe animation and are ready to begin experimenting with your own projects. Have fun!

Web Button Rollovers

When you hover over a button on a website, you'll often see that button change colour or glow. When you click the button, it'll often appear as though you've physically 'pushed' it. So, how do designers do this? Well, it's all controlled by a clever bit of code and different graphics known as **rollover states**. Not a programmer? That's fine, as DrawPlus creates all of the code for you!

By the end of this tutorial you will be able to:

- Create slice objects and set their properties.

- Preview your finished web button in a web browser.

- Export your web button and its rollover states.

So that we can get straight to the business end of creating a rollover button, we have created the starting button for you to download. However, if you are feeling adventurous, why not try creating your own using the steps outlined in the **Gel Button** tutorial?

 Go to **http://go.serif.com/resources/DPX4** to download the following tutorial project file(s):

🌐 **button.dpp**

Let's begin...

- In the Startup Wizard, choose **Open Saved Work**.

- Locate **button.dpp** and click **Open**.

 For this project, we have used a custom page setup with the ruler units set to pixels. Setting a specific page size is a good habit to get into when you are designing for a particular output such as for web buttons, icons and even logos. For more on changing ruler units and setting page size, see online Help.

The button displayed in the workspace will become our **normal** rollover state i.e., the image that people will see first when the button is placed on a web page. The next step is to create the variant states. To do this, we need to create a sliced object. Let's do this now.

To create and adjust a sliced object:

1   On the **Insert** menu, click **Web Object>Image Slice**.

2   With the ⁺∕ cursor, click and drag over the button to set the approximate size of the slice object.

On release, slice lines are displayed on the page defining the
button as a separate web object.

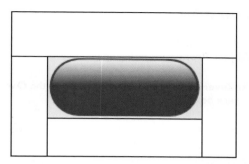

3   Click the **Pointer Tool**, then drag the handles of the slice
object so that they line up with the edges of the image.

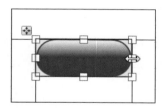

A quick way of inserting a slice object is from the right-click menu. Select your
button first, and then on the right-click menu, click **Insert Slice Object**. The slice
area is immediately created at the correct size for the object.

Now that our button is defined as a web object, we need to define its rollover states. This will allow us to apply different graphics to each state.

To define rollover states:

1   Double-click the shaded region of the slice object. The **Image Slice Object Properties** dialog opens.

2   In the **Rollover Details** section, click to select the **Over** and **Down** check boxes and click **OK**.

3   On the **Layers** tab, you'll now see four layers in the document:

  •   **Web Layer**—containing the image slice object.

  •   **Down**

  •   **Over**

  •   **Normal**—containing the button.

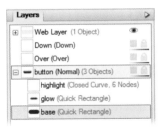

On the **Layers** tab, if you select the **Down** or **Over** layer, you'll see that they are empty. As we already have a graphic on our **Normal** layer, we can use this to create a **variant state** (a different graphic) on the **Over** and **Down** layers.

To create rollover states:

1   On the **Layers** tab, click 👁 to hide the **Web Layer**.

2   Click to select the 'button (**Normal**)' layer.

3   With the ⬉ **Pointer Tool**, drag a selection around the entire button, and press **Ctrl + C** to copy.

4   On the **Layers** tab, select the **Over** layer. Press **Ctrl + V** to paste the copied objects. An exact copy of the objects is pasted in place.

5   Next, click to select the **Down** layer. Press **Ctrl + V** to paste the copied objects to this layer also.

You should now have an exact copy of the button on each of the three 'state' layers (which you can see by expanding each layer as we have done).

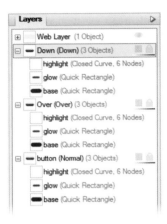

As each state is an exact copy, we wouldn't see any change when we hovered over the button. As this would be pointless, we need to create a different image for each state. The easiest way to do this is to change the colour of the button. We'll do this now.

 For the following steps, we'll assume that you are familiar with changing the fill colour of an object. If you need to review this, please see the **Fills I** and **Fills II** tutorials.

6   On the **Layers** tab, select the **Over** layer and then, click the **glow** object.

7   On the **Colour** tab, adjust the colour wheel to apply a lighter fill.

8   Next, select the **Down** layer and this time, click the **base** object, and on the **Colour** tab, adjust the colour wheel to apply a lighter fill.

9   Next, click the **glow** object, and on the **Colour** tab, adjust the colour wheel to apply a suitable fill.

Now that our three states are complete, we can preview the button in a web browser.

To preview a button:

1   On the **File** menu, click **Preview in Browser**. This launches your default browser and displays the button.

2   Roll your mouse over the button and click to see the variant 'Over' and 'Down' graphics you defined.

3   Close the browser window when you have finished previewing your button.

When you click the button, you'll almost certainly get an error message. This is because there is no URL link specified for the button. We'll show you how to set a link and specify some rollover text now...

 Don't forget to save your work!

To apply button actions:

1   On the **Layers** tab, select the **Web Layer** and click ⬤ to make it visible.

2   Right-click the shaded region of the slice object and click **Properties...** The **Image Slice Object Properties** dialog opens.

3   In the URL details section:

• Type a URL for your button to point to (for example www.drawplus.com).

• Type some descriptive text. This will appear when you point to the button. (For example 'visit drawplus.com!)

• Click **OK**.

4   Preview you button again to see the changes in action.

To export the complete rollover button:

1   On the **Web** layer, select the slice object and on the **File** menu, click **Export > Export as Image...**

2   In the **Export Optimizer** dialog:

- In the **Export Area** section, click **Selected Area**.

- In the **Properties** section, in the **Format** drop-down list, select an appropriate file type (typically GIF, JPEG, or PNG) and choose your settings. (We selected **32 bit PNG**).

- In the **Web Options** section, select the **Image Slices** check box.

- Click **Export**.

3   In the **Export** dialog, select a location for your exported files (we recommend creating a folder first). Type a name for your button (e.g., btn) and click **Save**.

Congratulations, you've exported your web button along with its rollover states!

DrawPlus creates a file for each image state, and a single file containing the HTML code, from which you can copy and paste <head> and <body> sections into the corresponding sections of your web page.

If you now open your folder, the contents should resemble ours. (The appearance of the files depends on your settings and your current default browser—in our case, we have file extensions visible and the default browser is FireFox.)

Name	Size	Date modified
btn.html Firefox Document 3.85 KB		btn.png PNG File 2.57 KB
btn_d.png PNG File 2.69 KB		btn_h.png PNG File 2.92 KB

DrawPlus
Gallery

This chapter showcases the content provided on the DrawPlus X4 **Gallery** tab. You'll find clipart, layout symbols, connecting symbols, shape art, and more.

Gallery items are organized into **Clipart**, **Home**, **Office**, **School** and **Shape Art** categories.

Clipart

Animals

Bird	Bumblebee	Cow	Crab	Crocodile
Dinosaur	Dog	Donkey	Dove	Eagle
Elephant	Frog	Giraffe	Goldfish	Hamster
Hedgehog	Hippopotamus	Horse	Killer Whale	Ladybird
Lion	Lizard	Monkey	Mouse	Owl Baby

Owl

Penguin

Pig

Rabbit

Rat

Rhinoceros

Rooster

Shark

Sheep

Snake

Spider

Starfish

Tiger

Whale

 Birth

Baby

Bib for Boy

Bib for Girl

Bootie

Bottle

Boy Girl Symbol

Pacifier

Rattle

Romper Suit

Sock

Teddy	Baby Bottle	Baby Mobile	Boy's Baby Rattle	Boy's Baby Booties
Butterfly	Flower	Girl's Baby Rattle	Girl's Booties	Moon
Rocking Bed	Star	Stork for Boy	Stork for Girl	Teddy Bear

Christmas

Purple Bauble	Orange Bauble	Candy Cane	Christmas Tree	Decorated Christmas Tree

Christmas Trees	More Christmas Trees	Elf	Fairy	Holly

Orange Bauble 2

Penguin Fairy

Penguin on Tree

Penguin with Balloons

Penguin with Cake

Penguin with Party Hat

Penguins and Tinsel

Polar Bear

Purple Bauble 2

Purple Present

Red Present

Robin

Santa with Presents

Bell

Candle

Holly

Mistletoe

Rudolph

Rudolph 2

Scroll Banner

Stocking

Wreath

Pudding

Angel

Angel 2

Wreath

Bauble

Baby Jesus

Wise Man

Stocking

Holly 02   Snowman   Sugar Cane   Robin 02   Crown

Cracker   Mistletoe 02   Reindeer   Shepherd   Simple Tree

Gift   Santa

Easter

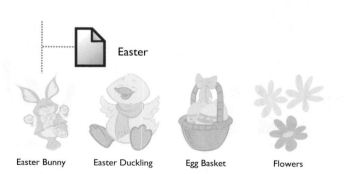

Easter Bunny   Easter Duckling   Egg Basket   Flowers

Fashion

Boots

Brush

Champagne Bottle

Champagne Glasses

Eyelash Brush

Flowers in Vase

Flowers

Gold Perfume Bottle

Green Perfume Bottle

Hair Brush

Hairdryer

Handbag

Hat

High Heels

Lipstick

Make-Up Brush

Mirror 1

Mirror 2

Perfume

Platform Shoes

Shoes

Slippers

Spray

Star

Bathtime

Shopping Girl

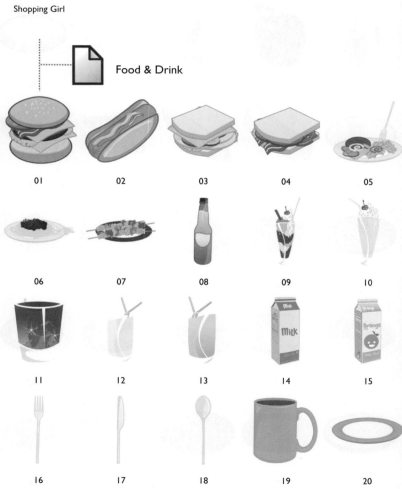

Food & Drink

01	02	03	04	05
06	07	08	09	10
11	12	13	14	15
16	17	18	19	20

21

22

23

24

25

26

27

28

29

30

31

32

33

34

35

36

37

38

39

40

41

42

43

44

45

46

47

48

49

50

51

52

53

54

55

56

57

58

59

60

61

62

63

64

65

66

67

68

69

70

71

72

73

74

75

76

77

78

79

80

81	82	83	84	85
86	87	88	89	90
91	92	93	94	95

Funny Faces

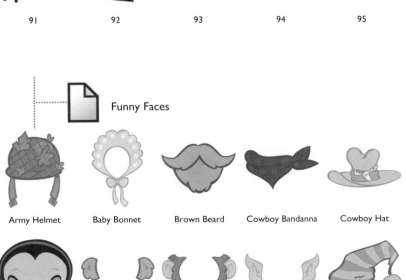

| Army Helmet | Baby Bonnet | Brown Beard | Cowboy Bandanna | Cowboy Hat |
| Dracula | Ear Warmers | Ears | Elf Ears | Elf Hat |

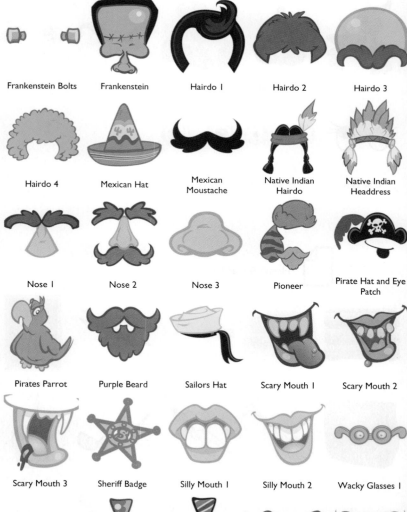

Frankenstein Bolts	Frankenstein	Hairdo 1	Hairdo 2	Hairdo 3
Hairdo 4	Mexican Hat	Mexican Moustache	Native Indian Hairdo	Native Indian Headdress
Nose 1	Nose 2	Nose 3	Pioneer	Pirate Hat and Eye Patch
Pirates Parrot	Purple Beard	Sailors Hat	Scary Mouth 1	Scary Mouth 2
Scary Mouth 3	Sheriff Badge	Silly Mouth 1	Silly Mouth 2	Wacky Glasses 1

Wacky Glasses 2	Wacky Tie 1	Wacky Tie 2	Wacky Tie 3	Werewolf

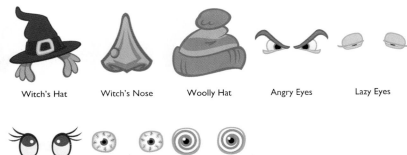

Witch's Hat   Witch's Nose   Woolly Hat   Angry Eyes   Lazy Eyes

Cute Eyes   Blood-shot Eyes   Hypnotic Eyes

Home & Garden

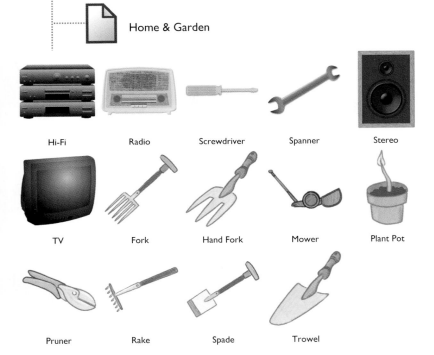

Hi-Fi   Radio   Screwdriver   Spanner   Stereo

TV   Fork   Hand Fork   Mower   Plant Pot

Pruner   Rake   Spade   Trowel

Party

Balloon

Balloons

Bottle Cork

Champagne

Cupcake

Party Blower

Party Hat

Party Popper

People & Professions

Waitress

Police Officer

Superhero

Secretary

Girl

Boy

Tennis Player

Butler

Firefighter

Scientist

Golfer

Businessman

Professor

Builder

Businessman

Chef

Fireman

Nurse

Policeman

Spaceman

Teacher

School Girl

School Boy

Butcher

Doctor

Fire Officer

Mechanic

Paramedic

Plumber

Policeman

Postman

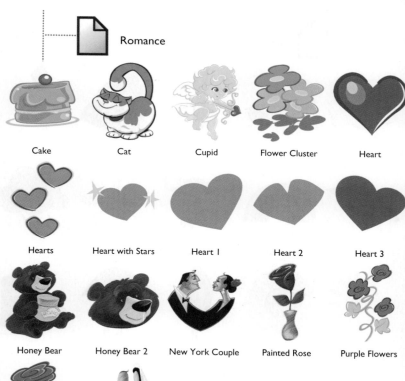

Romance

Cake

Cat

Cupid

Flower Cluster

Heart

Hearts

Heart with Stars

Heart 1

Heart 2

Heart 3

Honey Bear

Honey Bear 2

New York Couple

Painted Rose

Purple Flowers

Rose

Wedding Figures

Seasons

Clouds

Glove

Grass

Hat

Kit

Leaf

Rainbow

Scarf

Snowflake

Storm

Sun

Sunflower

Tree

Umbrella

Wellies

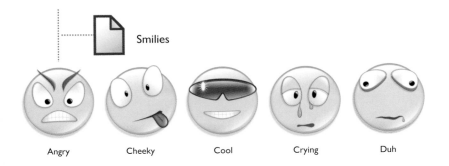

Smilies

Angry

Cheeky

Cool

Crying

Duh

Grin	Rich	Romance	Sleepy	Surprise

Sports & Leisure

8 Ball	Bowling Ball	Basketball	Tennis Ball	Soccer Ball
Ball	Puck	Football	Bowling Pin	Drinks Bottle
Baseball Bat	Hockey Stick	Gold Cup	Silver Cup	Gold Medal
Silver Medal	Boxing Gloves	Discus	Hammer	Tennis Racket

Goggles

Football Helmet

Baseball Helmet

Locker

Skis

Snowboard

Ice Hockey Stick

Golf Club

Pool Cue

Boxer

Rugby Player

Tennis Player

Baseball Field

Basketball Court

Chess Board

Cricket Strip

Soccer Pitch

Hockey Pitch

Pool Table

Tennis Court

Tennis Court

Benchpress

Weights 01

Skipping Rope

Watch Stop

Trampoline

Treadmill

Weights 02

Arrow 01

Circle

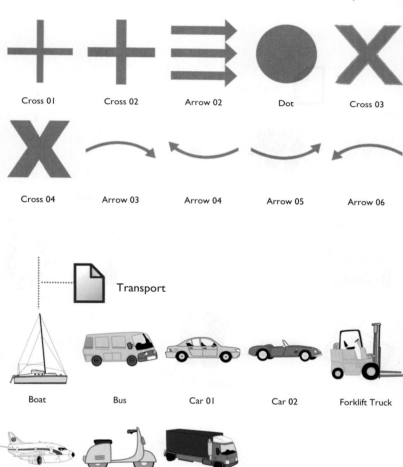

Cross 01

Cross 02

Arrow 02

Dot

Cross 03

Cross 04

Arrow 03

Arrow 04

Arrow 05

Arrow 06

Transport

Boat

Bus

Car 01

Car 02

Forklift Truck

Jet

Scooter

Truck

Wedding

Bells

Bouquet

Bride

Bridesmaids Dress

Cake

Church

Dress

Garter

Groom

Horseshoe

Just Married Sign

Limousine

Top Hat

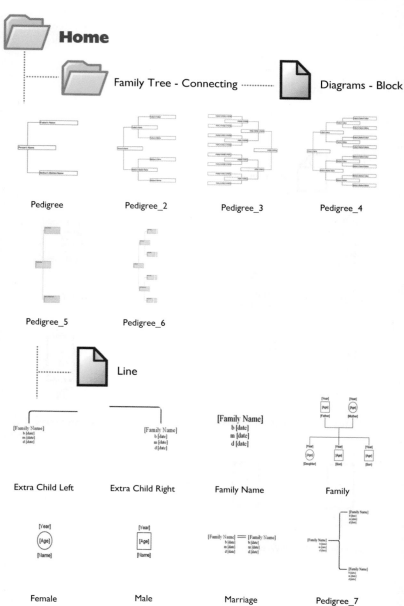

Home

Family Tree - Connecting .... Diagrams - Block

Pedigree

Pedigree_2

Pedigree_3

Pedigree_4

Pedigree_5

Pedigree_6

Line

Extra Child Left

Extra Child Right

Family Name

Family

Female

Male

Marriage

Pedigree_7

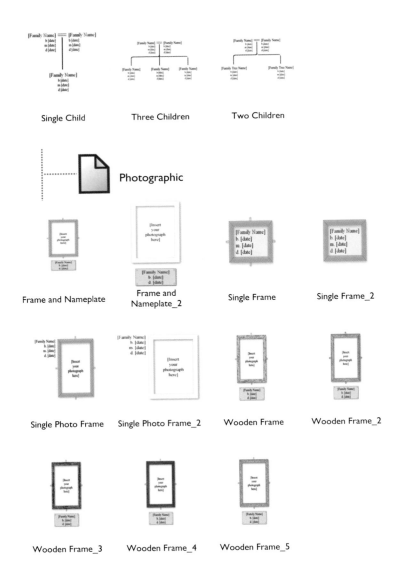

Single Child

Three Children

Two Children

Photographic

Frame and Nameplate

Frame and Nameplate_2

Single Frame

Single Frame_2

Single Photo Frame

Single Photo Frame_2

Wooden Frame

Wooden Frame_2

Wooden Frame_3

Wooden Frame_4

Wooden Frame_5

Fun & Crafts .... Badges

Rainbow   Skull   Boy   Girl   I Love You

Mod   Punk   Smile   Pop   Star

Rock   Flaming Bike   Seal   Dice   Butterflies

Flower   Fire   Car

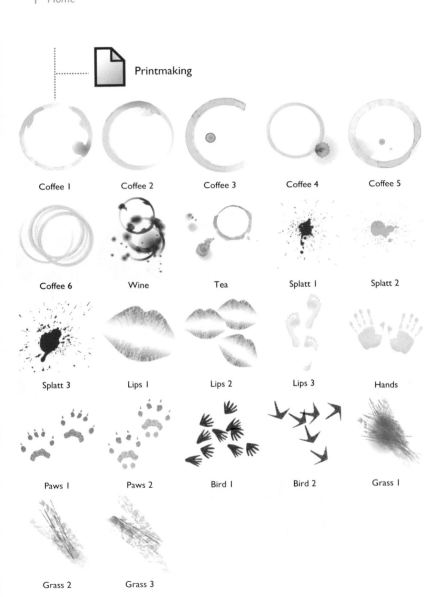

Printmaking

Coffee 1   Coffee 2   Coffee 3   Coffee 4   Coffee 5

Coffee 6   Wine   Tea   Splatt 1   Splatt 2

Splatt 3   Lips 1   Lips 2   Lips 3   Hands

Paws 1   Paws 2   Bird 1   Bird 2   Grass 1

Grass 2   Grass 3

Scrapbooking

Tag	Price	Pin	Yellow Note	Pin
Sticker	Price	Polaroid	Paper Clip	Paper
Pink Note	Yellow Note	Page Curl	Page Corner	Pin
Tag	Label	Paper	Note	Old Label
Tape Measure	Safety Pins	Buttons	Sequins	Jewels

Glass Beads

Flower Beads

Furry Teddies

Furry Sun

Furry Flowers

Furry Dogs

Boggly Eyes

 Stickers

Blue Stars

Party Rabbit

Sun Cocktail

White Rabbit

Party Cat

Orange Sweets

Strawberry Cream

Golden Rabbit

Mint Sweets

Ice Cream

Blue Cat

Vanilla Cream

Vanilla Cherry

Raspberry Radio

Red Rabbit

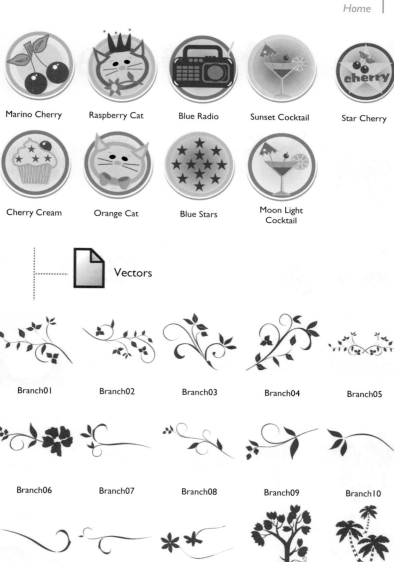

Marino Cherry

Raspberry Cat

Blue Radio

Sunset Cocktail

Star Cherry

Cherry Cream

Orange Cat

Blue Stars

Moon Light
Cocktail

Vectors

Branch01

Branch02

Branch03

Branch04

Branch05

Branch06

Branch07

Branch08

Branch09

Branch10

Branch11

Branch12

Branch13

Branch14

Branch15

Branch16

Floral01

Floral02

Floral03

Floral04

Floral05

Floral06

Floral07

Floral08

Floral09

Floral10

Floral11

Decorative01

Decorative02

Decorative03

Decorative04

Decorative05

Decorative06

Decorative07

Motif01

Motif02

Motif03

Motif04

Motif05

Motif06

Motif07

Motif08

Motif09

Motif10

Twirl01

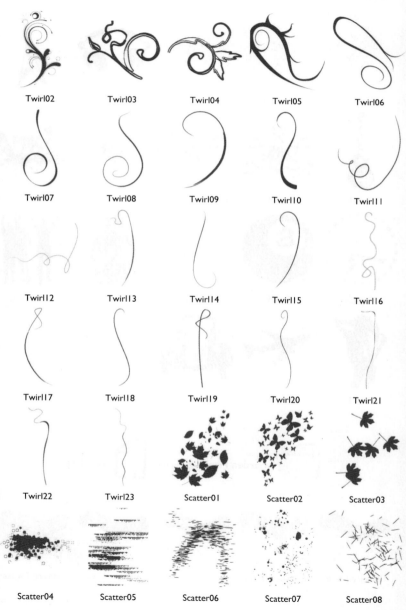

Twirl02 Twirl03 Twirl04 Twirl05 Twirl06

Twirl07 Twirl08 Twirl09 Twirl10 Twirl11

Twirl12 Twirl13 Twirl14 Twirl15 Twirl16

Twirl17 Twirl18 Twirl19 Twirl20 Twirl21

Twirl22 Twirl23 Scatter01 Scatter02 Scatter03

Scatter04 Scatter05 Scatter06 Scatter07 Scatter08

Scatter09   Scatter10   Scatter11   Pop01   Pop02

Pop03   Pop04   Pop05   Pop06   Pop07

Pop08   Pop09   Pop10   Pop11   Pop12

Pop13   Aeroplane   Car

Garden Planning .... Bedding

Bedding 1 blue   Bedding 1 mauve   Bedding 1 pink   Bedding 1 red   Bedding 1 white

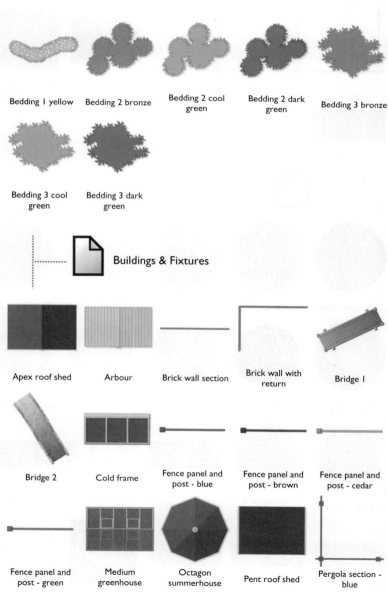

Bedding 1 yellow

Bedding 2 bronze

Bedding 2 cool green

Bedding 2 dark green

Bedding 3 bronze

Bedding 3 cool green

Bedding 3 dark green

Buildings & Fixtures

Apex roof shed

Arbour

Brick wall section

Brick wall with return

Bridge 1

Bridge 2

Cold frame

Fence panel and post - blue

Fence panel and post - brown

Fence panel and post - cedar

Fence panel and post - green

Medium greenhouse

Octagon summerhouse

Pent roof shed

Pergola section - blue

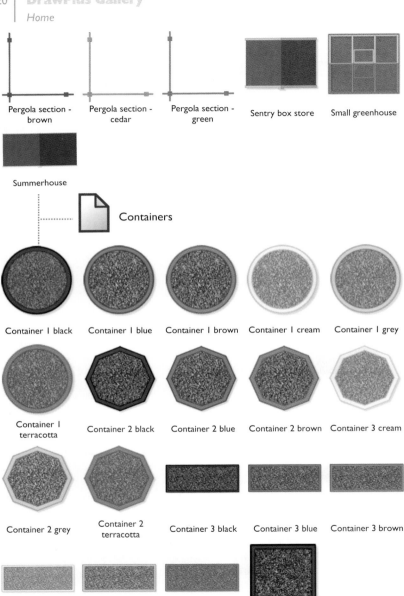

Pergola section - brown

Pergola section - cedar

Pergola section - green

Sentry box store

Small greenhouse

Summerhouse

Containers

Container 1 black

Container 1 blue

Container 1 brown

Container 1 cream

Container 1 grey

Container 1 terracotta

Container 2 black

Container 2 blue

Container 2 brown

Container 3 cream

Container 2 grey

Container 2 terracotta

Container 3 black

Container 3 blue

Container 3 brown

Container 3 cream

Container 3 grey

Container 3 terracotta

Container 4 black

Container 4 blue

Container 4 brown

Container 4 cream

Container 4 grey

Container 4 terracotta

Furniture

Barbecue

Blue patio chair

Blue patio table 1

Blue patio table 2

Blue patio table 3

Blue patio table 4

Blue patio umbrella

Garden seat

Gnome

Green patio umbrella

Kid's slide

Natural patio chair

Natural patio table 1

Natural patio table 2

Natural patio table 3

Natural patio table 4

Sandpit

Teak patio chair

Teak patio table 1

Teak patio table 2

Teak patio table 3

Teak patio table 4

Terrace seating
area - blue

Terrace seating
area - natural

Terrace seating
area - teak

Trampoline

Yellow patio
umbrella

Hedges, Shrubs & Trees

Hedge cool green

Hedge dark green

Large tree

Leylandii hedge

Medium tree

Shrub 1 cool green

Shrub 1 evergreen

Shrub 10 bronze

Shrub 10 cool
green

Shrub 10 dark
green

Shrub 2 bronze

Shrub 2 cool green

Shrub 2 dark green

Shrub 3 bronze

Shrub 3 cool green

Shrub 3 dark green

Shrub 4 bronze

Shrub 4 cool green

Shrub 4 dark green

Shrub 5 bronze

Shrub 5 cool green

Shrub 5 dark green

Shrub 6 dark green

Shrub 6 red-green

Shrub 6 silver grey

Shrub 7 cool green

Shrub 7 dark green

Shrub 7 yellow green

Shrub 8 blue

Shrub 8 mauve

Shrub 8 pink

Shrub 8 red

Shrub 8 white

Shrub 8 yellow

Shrub 9 bronze

Shrub 9 dark green

Shrub 9 pale green

Small tree

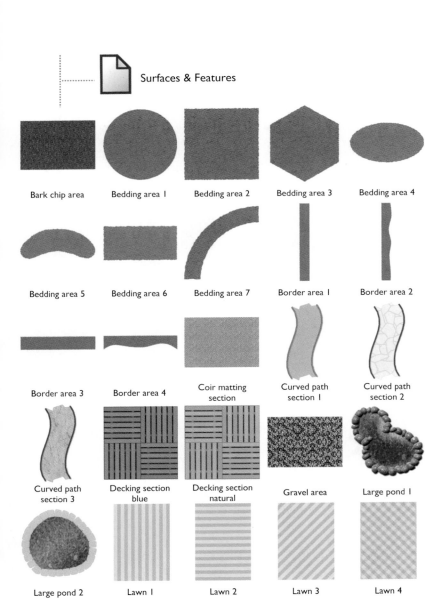

Surfaces & Features

Bark chip area

Bedding area 1

Bedding area 2

Bedding area 3

Bedding area 4

Bedding area 5

Bedding area 6

Bedding area 7

Border area 1

Border area 2

Border area 3

Border area 4

Coir matting
section

Curved path
section 1

Curved path
section 2

Curved path
section 3

Decking section
blue

Decking section
natural

Gravel area

Large pond 1

Large pond 2

Lawn 1

Lawn 2

Lawn 3

Lawn 4

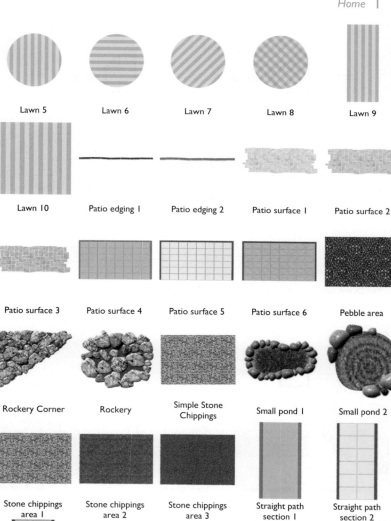

Lawn 5　　Lawn 6　　Lawn 7　　Lawn 8　　Lawn 9

Lawn 10　　Patio edging 1　　Patio edging 2　　Patio surface 1　　Patio surface 2

Patio surface 3　　Patio surface 4　　Patio surface 5　　Patio surface 6　　Pebble area

Rockery Corner　　Rockery　　Simple Stone Chippings　　Small pond 1　　Small pond 2

Stone chippings area 1　　Stone chippings area 2　　Stone chippings area 3　　Straight path section 1　　Straight path section 2

Straight path section 3

Stream 1

Stream 2

White sand area 2

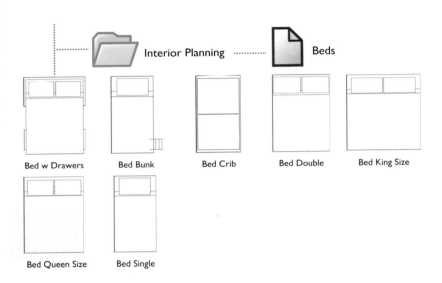

Interior Planning .... Beds

Bed w Drawers   Bed Bunk   Bed Crib   Bed Double   Bed King Size

Bed Queen Size   Bed Single

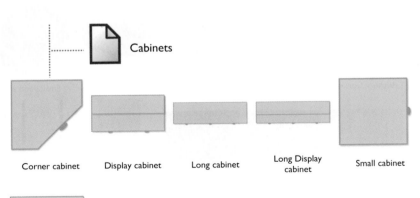

.... Cabinets

Corner cabinet   Display cabinet   Long cabinet   Long Display cabinet   Small cabinet

Wide cabinet

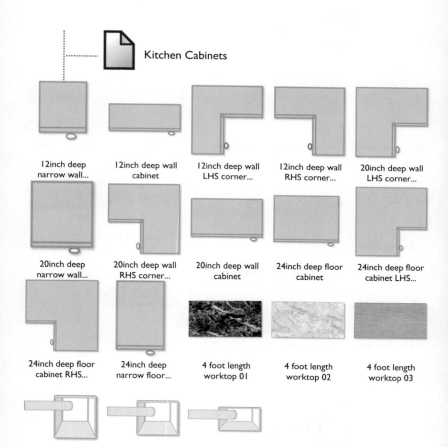

Kitchen Cabinets

12inch deep narrow wall...

12inch deep wall cabinet

12inch deep wall LHS corner...

12inch deep wall RHS corner...

20inch deep wall LHS corner...

20inch deep narrow wall...

20inch deep wall RHS corner...

20inch deep wall cabinet

24inch deep floor cabinet

24inch deep floor cabinet LHS...

24inch deep floor cabinet RHS...

24inch deep narrow floor...

4 foot length worktop 01

4 foot length worktop 02

4 foot length worktop 03

Extractor Hood 01

Extractor Hood 02

Extractor Hood 03

Leisure

Baby grand piano

Billiards table

Grand piano

Micro HiFi system

Midi HiFi system

Music keyboard

Portable TV

Record turntable

Standard HiFi system

Standard TV

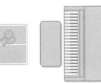

Table tennis table

Upright piano

VCR-DVD

Widescreen TV

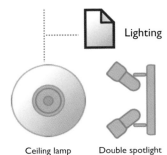

Lighting

Ceiling lamp

Double spotlight

Floor lamp with spots

Floor lamp

Low voltage spotlight

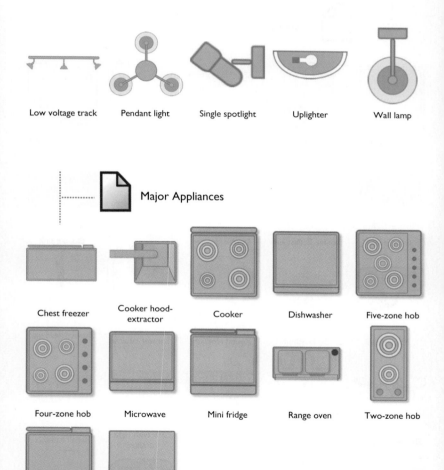

Low voltage track   Pendant light   Single spotlight   Uplighter   Wall lamp

Major Appliances

Chest freezer   Cooker hood-extractor   Cooker   Dishwasher   Five-zone hob

Four-zone hob   Microwave   Mini fridge   Range oven   Two-zone hob

Upright fridge-freezer   Washer or dryer

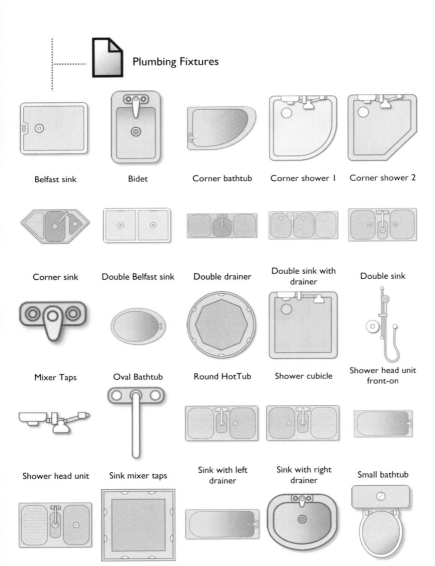

Plumbing Fixtures

Belfast sink

Bidet

Corner bathtub

Corner shower 1

Corner shower 2

Corner sink

Double Belfast sink

Double drainer

Double sink with drainer

Double sink

Mixer Taps

Oval Bathtub

Round HotTub

Shower cubicle

Shower head unit front-on

Shower head unit

Sink mixer taps

Sink with left drainer

Sink with right drainer

Small bathtub

Spacesaver sink

Square Hot Tub

Standard bathtub

Standard washbasin

Toilet with cistern

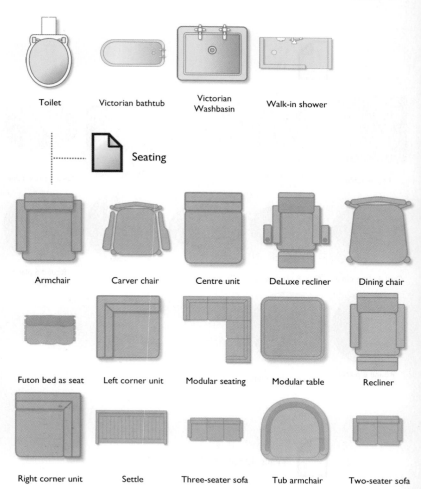

Toilet

Victorian bathtub

Victorian Washbasin

Walk-in shower

Seating

Armchair

Carver chair

Centre unit

DeLuxe recliner

Dining chair

Futon bed as seat

Left corner unit

Modular seating

Modular table

Recliner

Right corner unit

Settle

Three-seater sofa

Tub armchair

Two-seater sofa

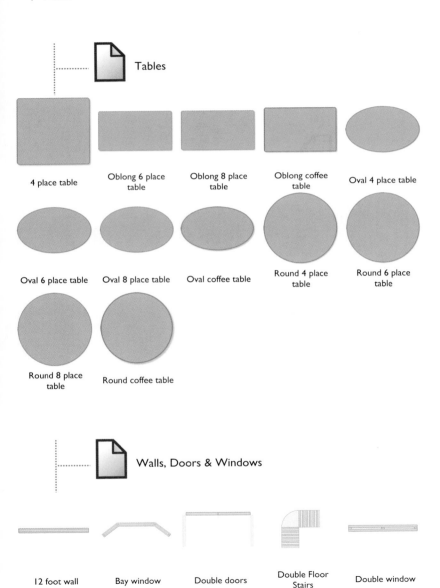

Tables

4 place table

Oblong 6 place table

Oblong 8 place table

Oblong coffee table

Oval 4 place table

Oval 6 place table

Oval 8 place table

Oval coffee table

Round 4 place table

Round 6 place table

Round 8 place table

Round coffee table

Walls, Doors & Windows

12 foot wall

Bay window

Double doors

Double Floor Stairs

Double window

Single window   Spiral Staircase   Stairs   Standard door -   Standard door -
                                                     left hand   right hand

Technical Planning

In the **Home** category you'll find a **Technical Planning** section, containing layout symbols that can be used for technical layout plans. Categories in this section are as follows:

- Building Fixtures
- Cabinets
- Cupboards
- Gardens
- Leisure
- Lighting
- Major Appliances
- Office Furniture
- Plumbing Fixtures
- Seating
- Tables

Office

Business Logos

Logo 01

Logo 02

Logo 03

Logo 04

Logo 05

Logo 06

Logo 07

Logo 08

Logo 09

Logo 10

Logo 11

Logo 12

Logo 13

Logo 14

Logo 15

Logo 16

Logo 17

Logo 18

Logo 19

Logo 20

Logo 21

Logo 22

Logo 23

Logo 24

Logo 25

Logo 26

Logo 27

Logo 28

Logo 29

Logo 30

Logo 31

Logo 32

Logo 33

Logo 34

Logo 35

Logo 36

Logo 37

Logo 38

Logo 39

Logo 40

Logo 41

Logo 42

Logo 43

Logo 44

Logo 45

Logo 46

Logo 47

Logo 48

Logo 49

Logo 50

Flowcharts - Connecting

Designed

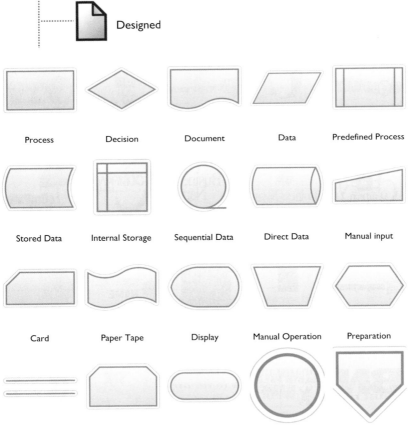

Process	Decision	Document	Data	Predefined Process
Stored Data	Internal Storage	Sequential Data	Direct Data	Manual input
Card	Paper Tape	Display	Manual Operation	Preparation
Parallel mode	Loop Limit	Terminator	On-page Reference	Off-page Reference

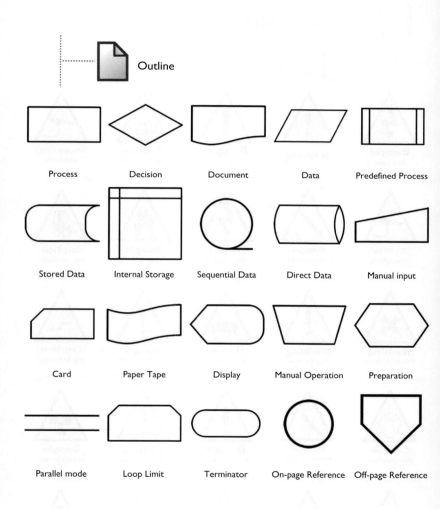

Outline

Process	Decision	Document	Data	Predefined Process
Stored Data	Internal Storage	Sequential Data	Direct Data	Manual input
Card	Paper Tape	Display	Manual Operation	Preparation
Parallel mode	Loop Limit	Terminator	On-page Reference	Off-page Reference

Health & Safety

 Hazard

415 Volts

Alarmed

Asbestos

Barbed Wire

Being Watched

CCTV

Compressed Gas

Electric Shock

Fire Risk

Fork Lift Trucks

Harmful Chemicals

Hot Water

Lorries Reversing

Men Working Overhead

Mind the Step

Mind your Head

Oxygen Cylinder

Persons at Work

Proceed with Care

Radiation Risk

Radiation

Ramps

Video Surveillance

Warning

Wet Floors

Mandatory

Angled Arrow

Arrow Up

Caretaker

Cloakroom

Computer Room

Enquiries

General Office

Keep Clear

Keep Out

Keep Shut

Library

Lift

Main Entrance

Meeting Room

Nursery

Private

Ramp

Reception

Report To

Ring for Assistance

Smoking Area

Smoking Room

Staff Only

Staff Room

Switch Off

Training Room

Waiting Room

Warning Sign

 Misc

QUALITY CONTROL
ACCEPTED

Accepted

QUALITY CONTROL
AWAITING
INSPECTION

Awaiting Inspection

Back Sign

DO NOT USE
UNTIL
CALIBRATION
COMPLETED

Calibration

CAR
PARK

Car Park

DATE INSTALLED

signed
dated

Date Installed

DELIVERIES

Deliveries

Directional Arrow

DO NOT
BEND

Do Not Bend

EMPLOYEE
PARKING

Employee Parking

ENTRANCE

Entrance

FRAGILE

Fragile

GOODS IN

Goods In

HANDLE
WITH CARE

Handle with Care

QUALITY CONTROL
ISO 9000

ISO 9000

⚠ Keep out

Keep Out

PRIVATE
PARKING

Private Parking

PRIVATE
PROPERTY

Private Property

comments

signed
dated

Quality Tested

QUALITY CONTROL
QUARANTINE
AREA

Quarantine Area

QUALITY CONTROL

REJECTED

Rejected

PLEASE RING FOR RECEPTION

Ring for Reception

PLEASE SWITCH OFF WHEN NOT IN USE

Switch Off

THIS SIDE UP

This Side Up

This Way Up

URGENT

Urgent

PLEASE USE OTHER DOOR

Use Other Door

VISITOR PARKING

Visitor Parking

 Prohibition

No cameras

Cameras

Do not disturb

Do Not Disturb

 Fire alarm

Fire Alarm

 Fire blanket

Fire Blanket

Left Arrow

Do not use mobile phones

Mobile Phone

 Motorcycle helmets must not be worn within these premises

Motorcycle

 No exit

No Exit

 No food or drink

No Food or Drink

 No Pedestrians

No Pedestrians

 No smoking

No Smoking

Standard

Assembly Point

Drinking Water

Eye Wash

Fire Exit 01

Fire Exit 02

First Aid Available

First Aid Post

First Aid

First Aiders

Left Arrow

Phone

Pull to Open

Pull

Push to Open

Push

Smoking Area

Networks - Connecting

Bridge

Camera

Cell Phone

Comm-link

Comm-link_2

CRT

CRT_2

Ethernet

Fax

Firewall

Hub

Modem

PC Unit

Photocopier

Printer

Projector

Router

Scanner

Screen

Switch

Telephone

TFT

User

Video Camera

Wireless Router

Wireless

Organisational Charts - Connecting

| Badge | Badge_2 | Badge_3 | Badge_4 | Badge_5 |

| Badge_6 | Badge_7 | Badge_8 | Circle | Circle_2 |

| Circle_3 | Circle_4 | Circle_5 | Circle_6 | Company Name |

| Company Name_2 | Company Name_3 | Company Name_4 | Company Name_5 | Company Name_6 |

| Company Name_6 | Lozenge | Lozenge_2 | Lozenge_3 | Lozenge_4 |

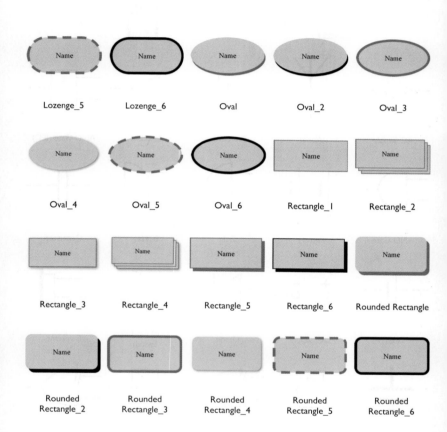

Lozenge_5   Lozenge_6   Oval   Oval_2   Oval_3

Oval_4   Oval_5   Oval_6   Rectangle_1   Rectangle_2

Rectangle_3   Rectangle_4   Rectangle_5   Rectangle_6   Rounded Rectangle

Rounded
Rectangle_2   Rounded
Rectangle_3   Rounded
Rectangle_4   Rounded
Rectangle_5   Rounded
Rectangle_6

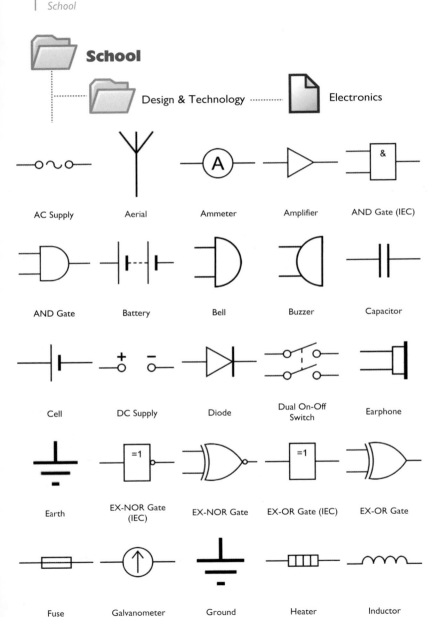

School

Design & Technology ········· Electronics

AC Supply

Aerial

Ammeter

Amplifier

AND Gate (IEC)

AND Gate

Battery

Bell

Buzzer

Capacitor

Cell

DC Supply

Diode

Dual On-Off Switch

Earphone

Earth

EX-NOR Gate (IEC)

EX-NOR Gate

EX-OR Gate (IEC)

EX-OR Gate

Fuse

Galvanometer

Ground

Heater

Inductor

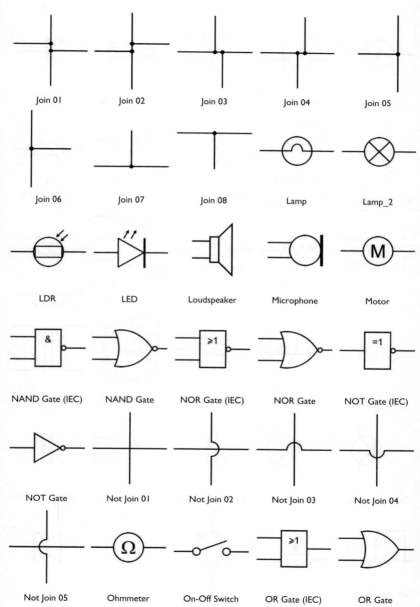

| Join 01 | Join 02 | Join 03 | Join 04 | Join 05 |

| Join 06 | Join 07 | Join 08 | Lamp | Lamp_2 |

| LDR | LED | Loudspeaker | Microphone | Motor |

| NAND Gate (IEC) | NAND Gate | NOR Gate (IEC) | NOR Gate | NOT Gate (IEC) |

| NOT Gate | Not Join 01 | Not Join 02 | Not Join 03 | Not Join 04 |

| Not Join 05 | Ohmmeter | On-Off Switch | OR Gate (IEC) | OR Gate |

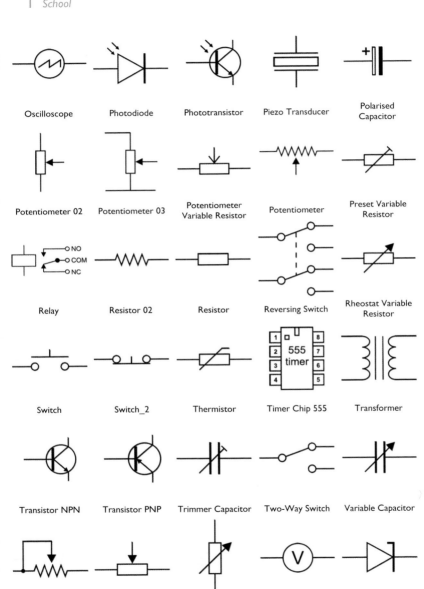

Oscilloscope	Photodiode	Phototransistor	Piezo Transducer	Polarised Capacitor
Potentiometer 02	Potentiometer 03	Potentiometer Variable Resistor	Potentiometer	Preset Variable Resistor
Relay	Resistor 02	Resistor	Reversing Switch	Rheostat Variable Resistor
Switch	Switch_2	Thermistor	Timer Chip 555	Transformer
Transistor NPN	Transistor PNP	Trimmer Capacitor	Two-Way Switch	Variable Capacitor
Variable Resistor 02	Variable Resistor 03	Variable Resistor	Voltmeter	Zener Diode

Food

Cake Knife

Chef Hat

Food Processor

Handheld Mixer

Knife

Rolling Pin

Salt & Pepper

Scales

Spoon

Toaster

Wooden Spoon

General

Cutting Board

Eraser

Hammer

Knife

Paintbrush

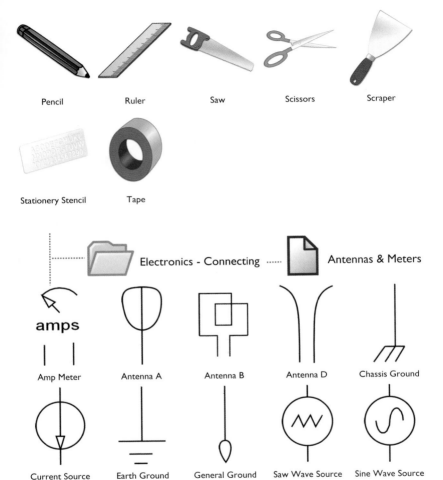

Pencil

Ruler

Saw

Scissors

Scraper

Stationery Stencil

Tape

Electronics - Connecting ...... Antennas & Meters

amps

Amp Meter

Antenna A

Antenna B

Antenna D

Chassis Ground

Current Source

Earth Ground

General Ground

Saw Wave Source

Sine Wave Source

Square Wave Source

volts

Volt Meter

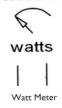

watts

Watt Meter

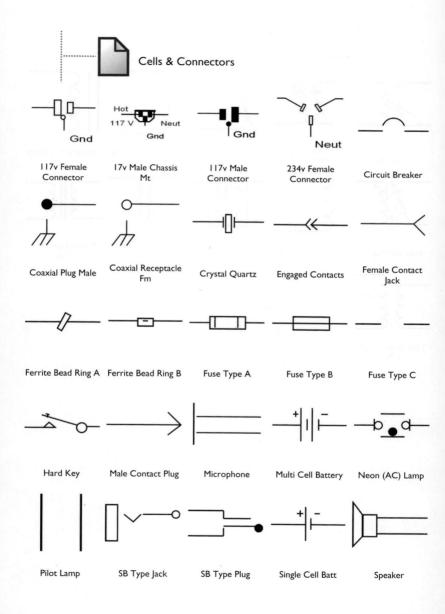

Cells & Connectors

Coils

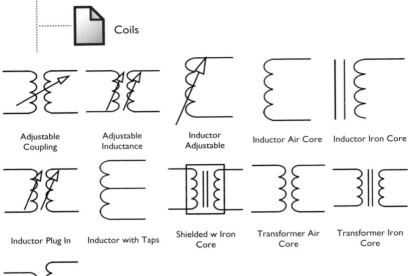

Adjustable Coupling	Adjustable Inductance	Inductor Adjustable	Inductor Air Core	Inductor Iron Core

Inductor Plug In	Inductor with Taps	Shielded w Iron Core	Transformer Air Core	Transformer Iron Core

Transformer with Link

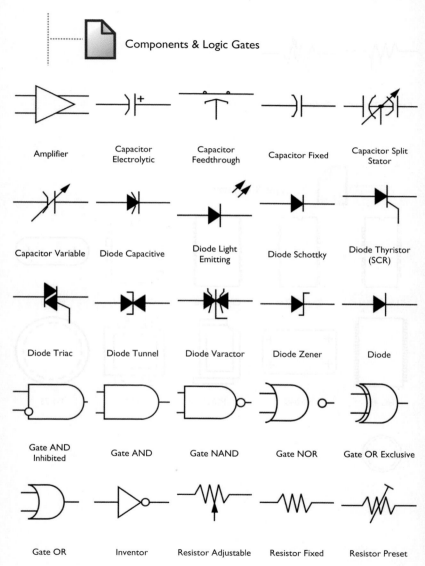

Components & Logic Gates

Amplifier

Capacitor Electrolytic

Capacitor Feedthrough

Capacitor Fixed

Capacitor Split Stator

Capacitor Variable

Diode Capacitive

Diode Light Emitting

Diode Schottky

Diode Thyristor (SCR)

Diode Triac

Diode Tunnel

Diode Varactor

Diode Zener

Diode

Gate AND Inhibited

Gate AND

Gate NAND

Gate NOR

Gate OR Exclusive

Gate OR

Inventor

Resistor Adjustable

Resistor Fixed

Resistor Preset

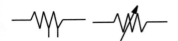

Resistor Tapped   Resistor Variable

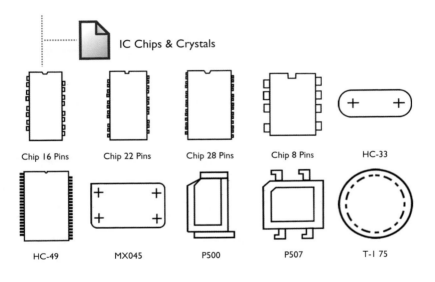

IC Chips & Crystals

Chip 16 Pins   Chip 22 Pins   Chip 28 Pins   Chip 8 Pins   HC-33

HC-49   MX045   P500   P507   T-1 75

T-1

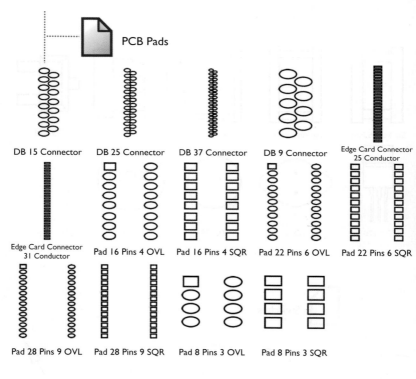

PCB Pads

DB 15 Connector   DB 25 Connector   DB 37 Connector   DB 9 Connector   Edge Card Connector
25 Conductor

Edge Card Connector
31 Conductor   Pad 16 Pins 4 OVL   Pad 16 Pins 4 SQR   Pad 22 Pins 6 OVL   Pad 22 Pins 6 SQR

Pad 28 Pins 9 OVL   Pad 28 Pins 9 SQR   Pad 8 Pins 3 OVL   Pad 8 Pins 3 SQR

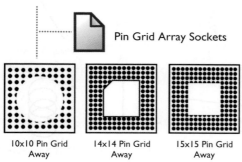

Pin Grid Array Sockets

10x10 Pin Grid
Away   14x14 Pin Grid
Away   15x15 Pin Grid
Away

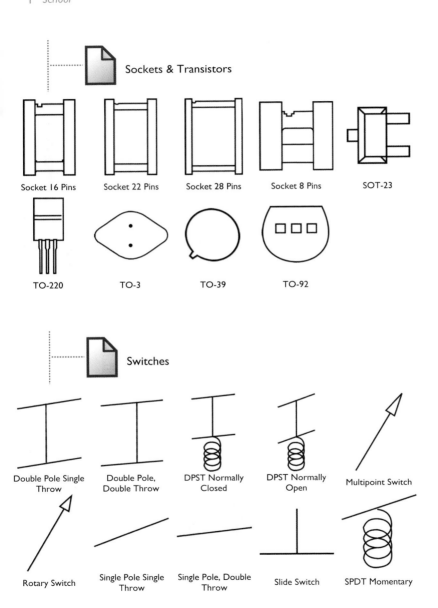

Sockets & Transistors

Socket 16 Pins

Socket 22 Pins

Socket 28 Pins

Socket 8 Pins

SOT-23

TO-220

TO-3

TO-39

TO-92

Switches

Double Pole Single Throw

Double Pole, Double Throw

DPST Normally Closed

DPST Normally Open

Multipoint Switch

Rotary Switch

Single Pole Single Throw

Single Pole, Double Throw

Slide Switch

SPDT Momentary

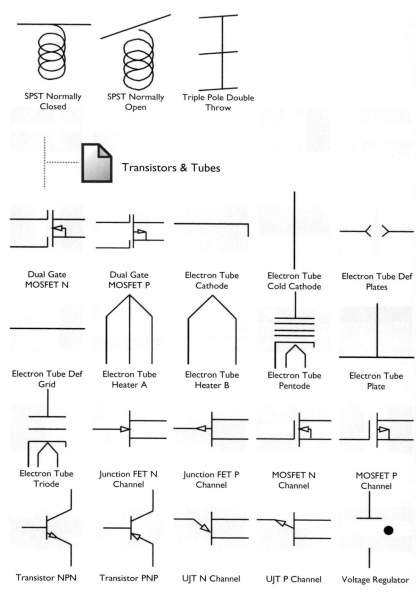

SPST Normally
Closed

SPST Normally
Open

Triple Pole Double
Throw

Transistors & Tubes

Dual Gate
MOSFET N

Dual Gate
MOSFET P

Electron Tube
Cathode

Electron Tube
Cold Cathode

Electron Tube Def
Plates

Electron Tube Def
Grid

Electron Tube
Heater A

Electron Tube
Heater B

Electron Tube
Pentode

Electron Tube
Plate

Electron Tube
Triode

Junction FET N
Channel

Junction FET P
Channel

MOSFET N
Channel

MOSFET P
Channel

Transistor NPN

Transistor PNP

UJT N Channel

UJT P Channel

Voltage Regulator

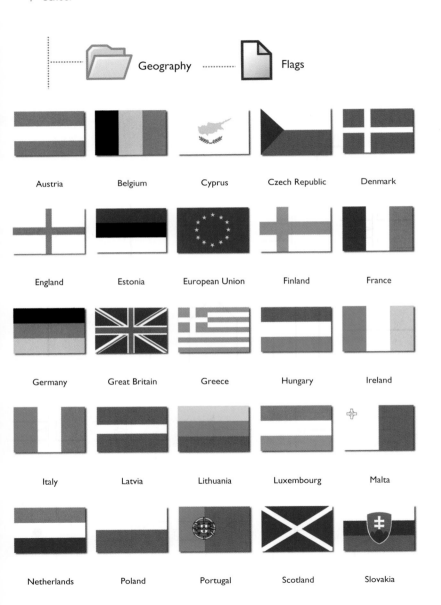

Geography .... Flags

Austria

Belgium

Cyprus

Czech Republic

Denmark

England

Estonia

European Union

Finland

France

Germany

Great Britain

Greece

Hungary

Ireland

Italy

Latvia

Lithuania

Luxembourg

Malta

Netherlands

Poland

Portugal

Scotland

Slovakia

Slovenia

Spain

Sweden

United States

Wales

Weather

Bright Slight
Clouds

Clouds some
Sunshine

Cloudy - Night

Cloudy

Dark Clouds with
Rain - Night

Dark Clouds with
Rain

Dark Clouds

Fog - Night

Hazy

Heavy Rain

Icy Blizzard - Night

Icy Blizzard

Lightening Storm -
Night

Lightening Storm

Mild Sunshine

Showers - Night

Showers

Snow - Night

Snow

Sunny Showers

Very Sunny

 Maths

 Colour

Abacus 01

Abacus 02

pi

Protractor

Ruler

Set Square

Set Square 02

Outline

Abacus 01

Abacus 02

pi

Protractor

Ruler

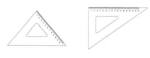

Set Square 01   Set Square 02

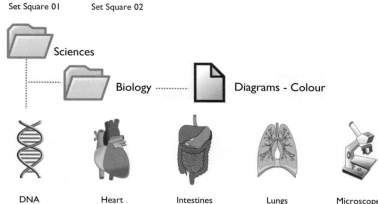

Sciences

Biology ·········· Diagrams - Colour

DNA   Heart   Intestines   Lungs   Microscope

Retina

Diagrams - Outline

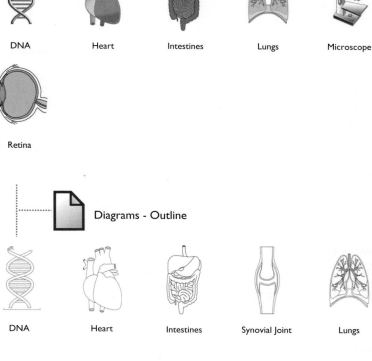

DNA   Heart   Intestines   Synovial Joint   Lungs

Microscope

Retina

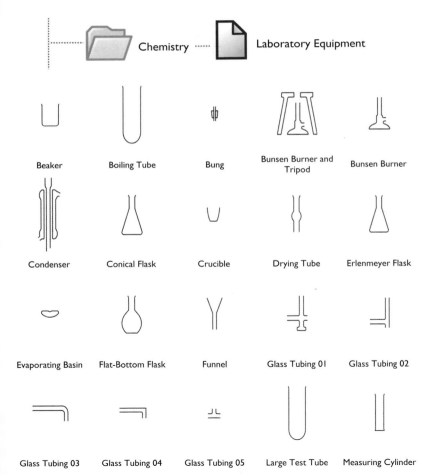

Chemistry .... Laboratory Equipment

Beaker

Boiling Tube

Bung

Bunsen Burner and Tripod

Bunsen Burner

Condenser

Conical Flask

Crucible

Drying Tube

Erlenmeyer Flask

Evaporating Basin

Flat-Bottom Flask

Funnel

Glass Tubing 01

Glass Tubing 02

Glass Tubing 03

Glass Tubing 04

Glass Tubing 05

Large Test Tube

Measuring Cylinder

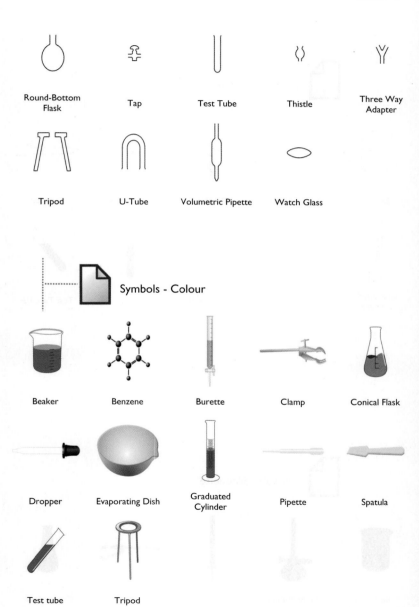

Round-Bottom Flask

Tap

Test Tube

Thistle

Three Way Adapter

Tripod

U-Tube

Volumetric Pipette

Watch Glass

Symbols - Colour

Beaker

Benzene

Burette

Clamp

Conical Flask

Dropper

Evaporating Dish

Graduated Cylinder

Pipette

Spatula

Test tube

Tripod

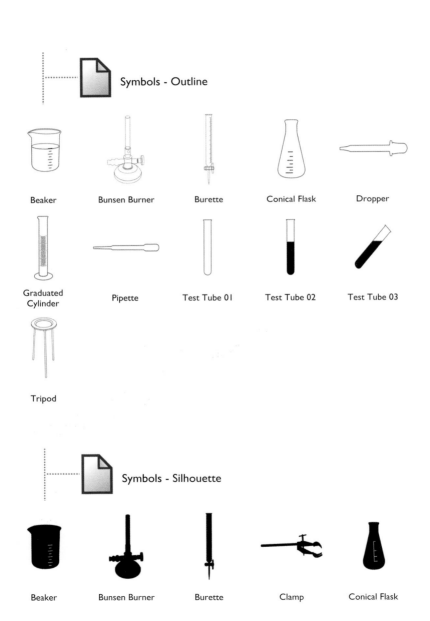

Symbols - Outline

Beaker

Bunsen Burner

Burette

Conical Flask

Dropper

Graduated
Cylinder

Pipette

Test Tube 01

Test Tube 02

Test Tube 03

Tripod

Symbols - Silhouette

Beaker

Bunsen Burner

Burette

Clamp

Conical Flask

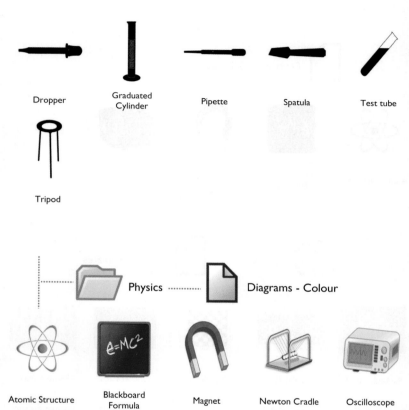

Dropper

Graduated Cylinder

Pipette

Spatula

Test tube

Tripod

Physics .... Diagrams - Colour

Atomic Structure

Blackboard Formula

Magnet

Newton Cradle

Oscilloscope

Telescope

Diagrams - Silhouette

Atomic Structure

Blackboard
Formula

Magnet

Oscilloscope

Sports .... Game Templates

BasketBall Pitch

BasketBall Court

Chess Board

Cricket Pitch

Football Pitch

Hockey Pitch

Rugby Pitch

Snooker Table

Tennis Clay Court

Tennis Grass
Court

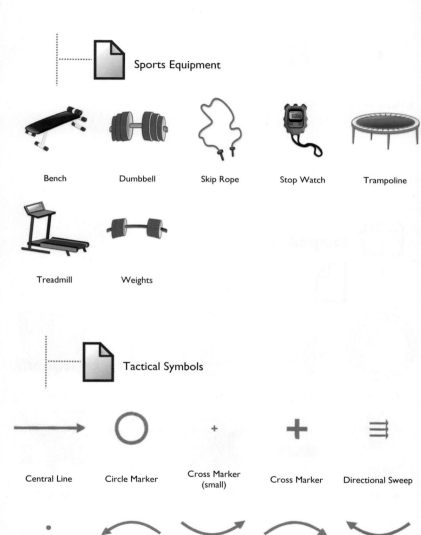

Sports Equipment

Bench

Dumbbell

Skip Rope

Stop Watch

Trampoline

Treadmill

Weights

Tactical Symbols

Central Line

Circle Marker

Cross Marker
(small)

Cross Marker

Directional Sweep

Player Marker

Wing Arrow
(down left)

Wing Arrow
(down right)

Wing Arrow (up
left)

Wing Arrow (up
right)

X Marker (small)   X Marker

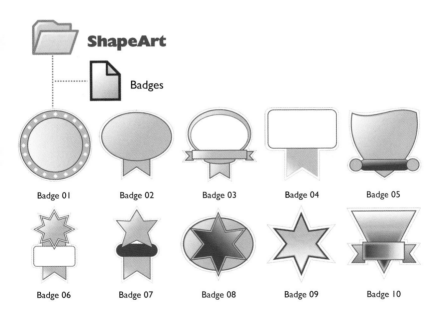

ShapeArt

Badges

Badge 01   Badge 02   Badge 03   Badge 04   Badge 05

Badge 06   Badge 07   Badge 08   Badge 09   Badge 10

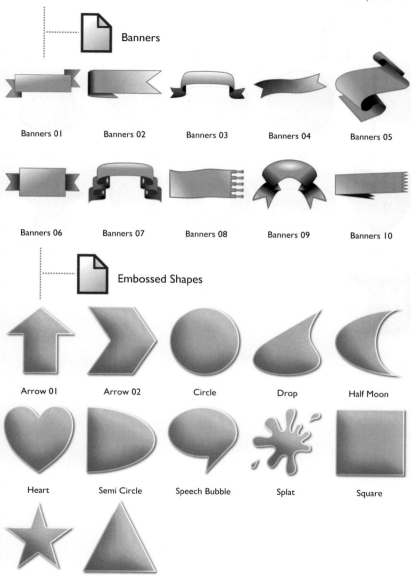

Banners

Banners 01

Banners 02

Banners 03

Banners 04

Banners 05

Banners 06

Banners 07

Banners 08

Banners 09

Banners 10

Embossed Shapes

Arrow 01

Arrow 02

Circle

Drop

Half Moon

Heart

Semi Circle

Speech Bubble

Splat

Square

Star

Triangle

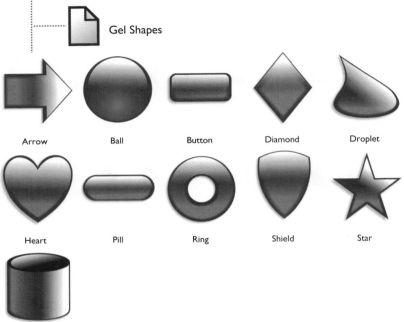

Gel Shapes

Arrow   Ball   Button   Diamond   Droplet

Heart   Pill   Ring   Shield   Star

Tube

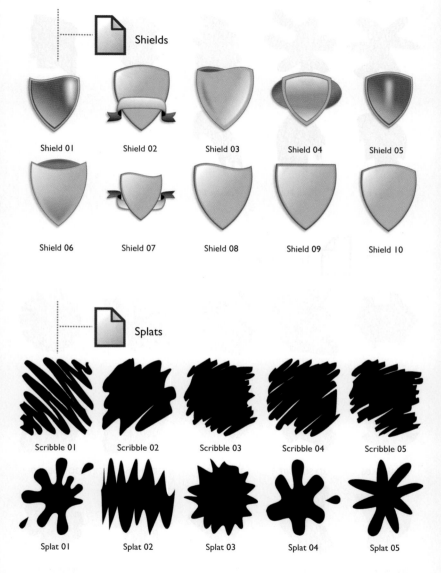

Shields

Shield 01

Shield 02

Shield 03

Shield 04

Shield 05

Shield 06

Shield 07

Shield 08

Shield 09

Shield 10

Splats

Scribble 01

Scribble 02

Scribble 03

Scribble 04

Scribble 05

Splat 01

Splat 02

Splat 03

Splat 04

Splat 05

| Splat 06 | Splat 07 | Splodge 01 | Splodge 02 | Splodge 03 |

| Splodge 04 | Splodge 05 | Splodge 06 |

 Third Dimension

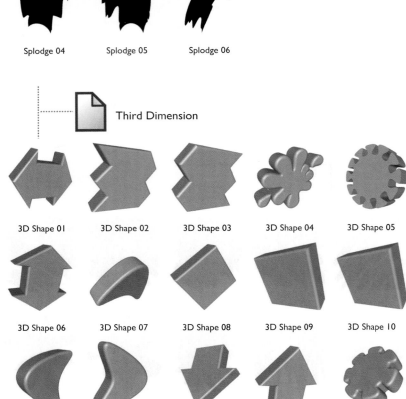

| 3D Shape 01 | 3D Shape 02 | 3D Shape 03 | 3D Shape 04 | 3D Shape 05 |

| 3D Shape 06 | 3D Shape 07 | 3D Shape 08 | 3D Shape 09 | 3D Shape 10 |

| 3D Shape 11 | 3D Shape 12 | 3D Shape 13 | 3D Shape 14 | 3D Shape 15 |

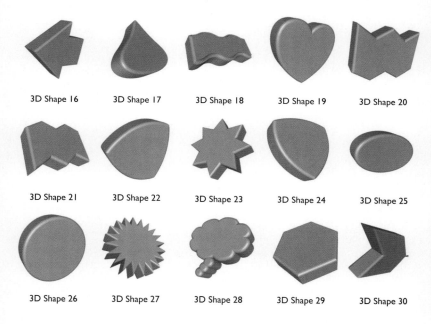

3D Shape 16   3D Shape 17   3D Shape 18   3D Shape 19   3D Shape 20

3D Shape 21   3D Shape 22   3D Shape 23   3D Shape 24   3D Shape 25

3D Shape 26   3D Shape 27   3D Shape 28   3D Shape 29   3D Shape 30

Effects

The **Effects** tab provides a wide selection of categorized preset effects that you can apply to objects on your page with a single click. Categories include **Glass, Glow, Marble, Metallic, Plastic**, and **Wood**.

 **Animals**

 Edible

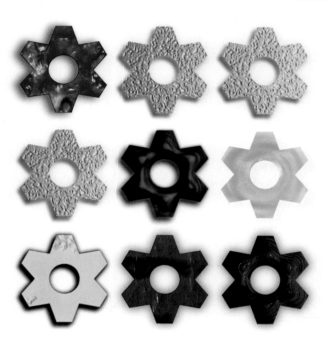

 Elements

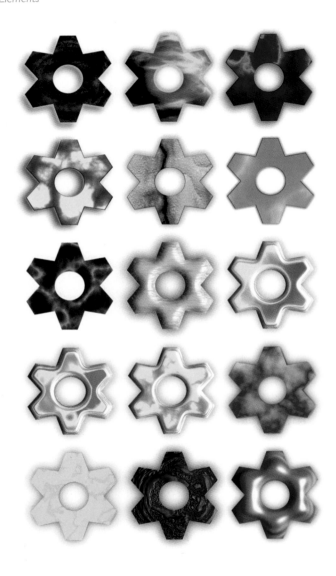

 Glass

 fx **Glow**

 Gross

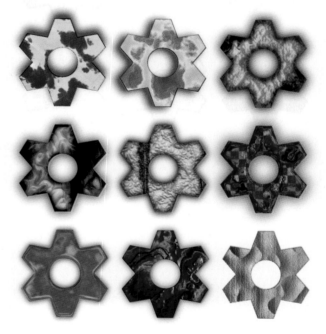

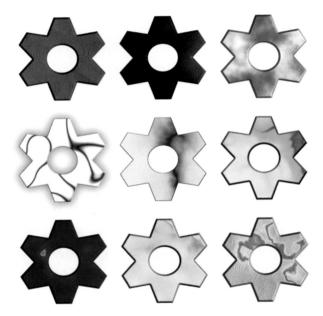

fx **Metallic**

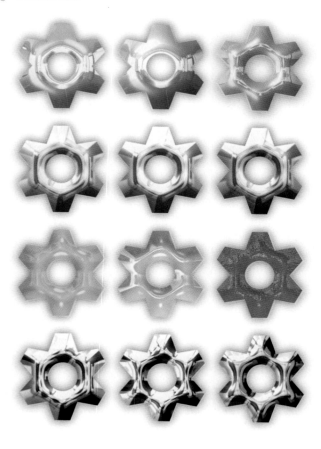

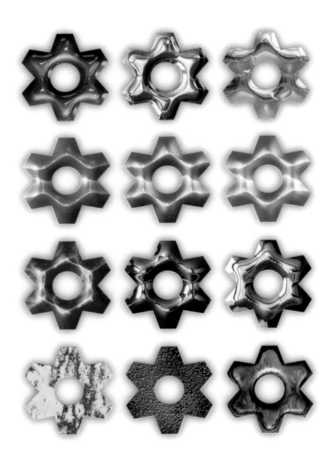

 **Organic**

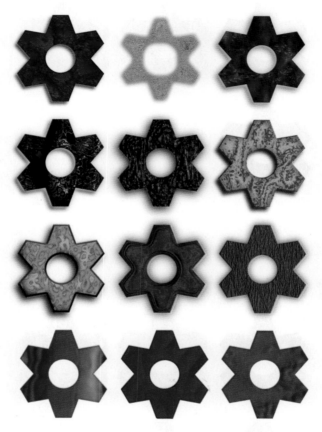

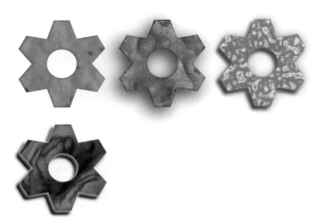

fx **Planetary**

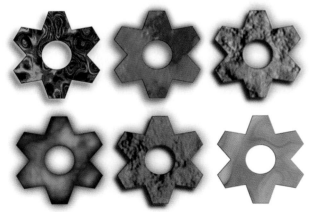

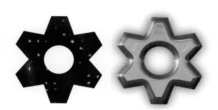

 Plastic

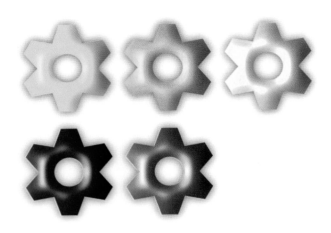

 ## Stone

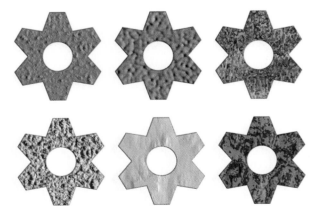

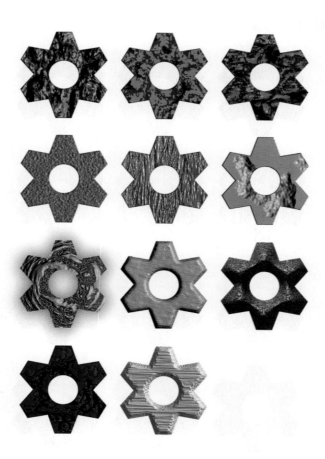

Wood

Brushes

DrawPlus provides an exciting range of possibilities for creating artistic effects using natural media effect brush strokes, spray brushes, coordinated themed palettes, and instant effects.

On the **Brushes** tab, you'll find a wide selection of new and improved brushes in **Draw**, **Edges**, **Effect**, **Embroidery**, **Grunge**, **Nature**, **Paint**, **Photo**, and **Spray** categories.

Why not try these out with DrawPlus X4's powerful **Pressure** tab functionality!

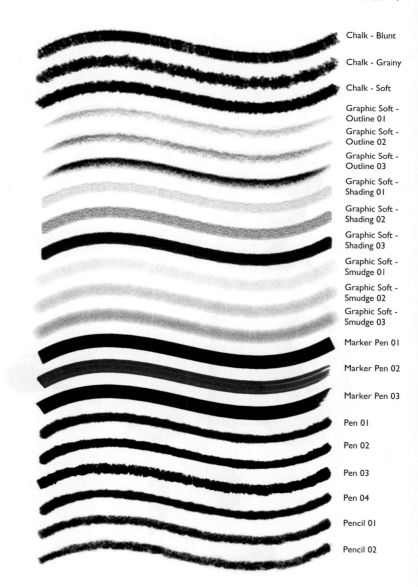

Chalk - Blunt

Chalk - Grainy

Chalk - Soft

Graphic Soft - Outline 01

Graphic Soft - Outline 02

Graphic Soft - Outline 03

Graphic Soft - Shading 01

Graphic Soft - Shading 02

Graphic Soft - Shading 03

Graphic Soft - Smudge 01

Graphic Soft - Smudge 02

Graphic Soft - Smudge 03

Marker Pen 01

Marker Pen 02

Marker Pen 03

Pen 01

Pen 02

Pen 03

Pen 04

Pencil 01

Pencil 02

This sample was created using the **Graphic Soft Shading** brushes, which you'll find in the **Brushes** tab's **Draw** category.

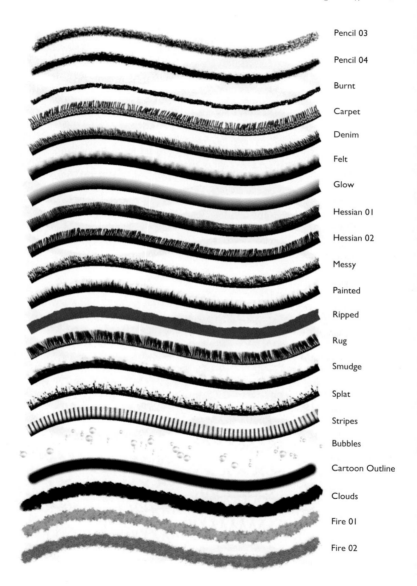

Pencil 03

Pencil 04

Burnt

Carpet

Denim

Felt

Glow

Hessian 01

Hessian 02

Messy

Painted

Ripped

Rug

Smudge

Splat

Stripes

Bubbles

Cartoon Outline

Clouds

Fire 01

Fire 02

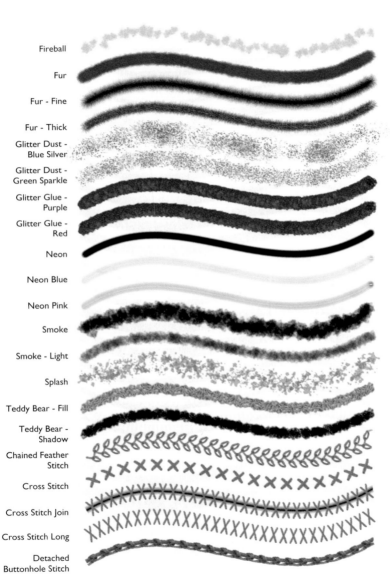

Fireball

Fur

Fur - Fine

Fur - Thick

Glitter Dust -
Blue Silver

Glitter Dust -
Green Sparkle

Glitter Glue -
Purple

Glitter Glue -
Red

Neon

Neon Blue

Neon Pink

Smoke

Smoke - Light

Splash

Teddy Bear - Fill

Teddy Bear -
Shadow

Chained Feather
Stitch

Cross Stitch

Cross Stitch Join

Cross Stitch Long

Detached
Buttonhole Stitch

This sample was made using the **Teddy Bear** brushes, located in the **Brushes** tab's **Effects** category.

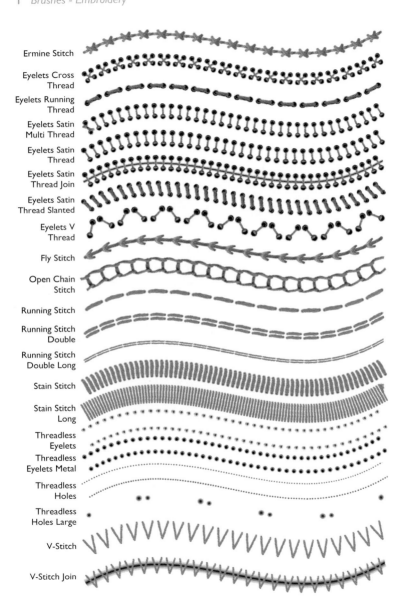

Ermine Stitch

Eyelets Cross Thread

Eyelets Running Thread

Eyelets Satin Multi Thread

Eyelets Satin Thread

Eyelets Satin Thread Join

Eyelets Satin Thread Slanted

Eyelets V Thread

Fly Stitch

Open Chain Stitch

Running Stitch

Running Stitch Double

Running Stitch Double Long

Stain Stitch

Stain Stitch Long

Threadless Eyelets

Threadless Eyelets Metal

Threadless Holes

Threadless Holes Large

V-Stitch

V-Stitch Join

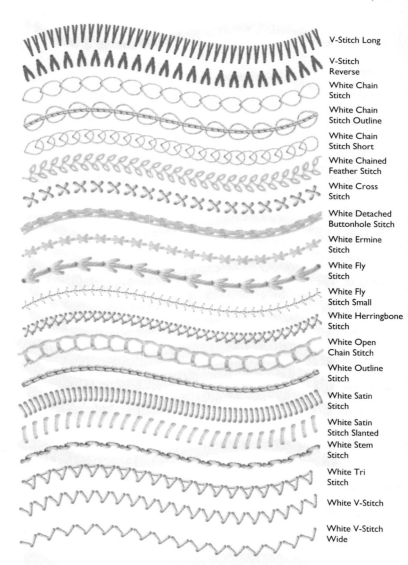

V-Stitch Long

V-Stitch Reverse

White Chain Stitch

White Chain Stitch Outline

White Chain Stitch Short

White Chained Feather Stitch

White Cross Stitch

White Detached Buttonhole Stitch

White Ermine Stitch

White Fly Stitch

White Fly Stitch Small

White Herringbone Stitch

White Open Chain Stitch

White Outline Stitch

White Satin Stitch

White Satin Stitch Slanted

White Stem Stitch

White Tri Stitch

White V-Stitch

White V-Stitch Wide

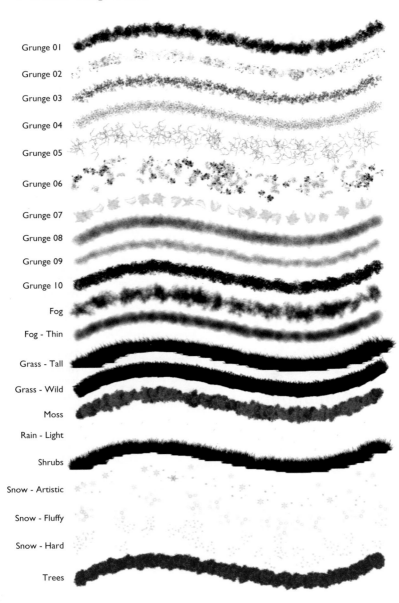

Grunge 01

Grunge 02

Grunge 03

Grunge 04

Grunge 05

Grunge 06

Grunge 07

Grunge 08

Grunge 09

Grunge 10

Fog

Fog - Thin

Grass - Tall

Grass - Wild

Moss

Rain - Light

Shrubs

Snow - Artistic

Snow - Fluffy

Snow - Hard

Trees

This sample was made using the **Trees** and **Fog** brushes.

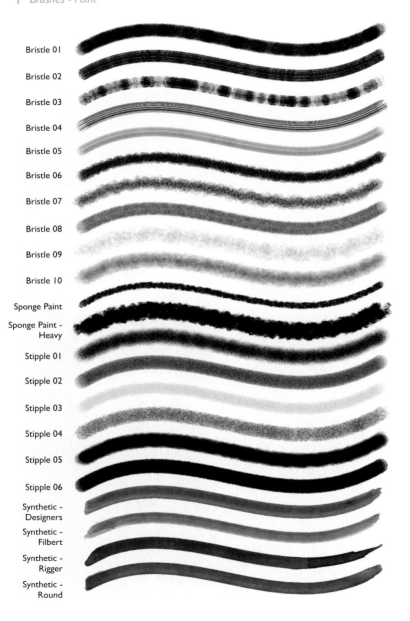

Bristle 01

Bristle 02

Bristle 03

Bristle 04

Bristle 05

Bristle 06

Bristle 07

Bristle 08

Bristle 09

Bristle 10

Sponge Paint

Sponge Paint - Heavy

Stipple 01

Stipple 02

Stipple 03

Stipple 04

Stipple 05

Stipple 06

Synthetic - Designers

Synthetic - Filbert

Synthetic - Rigger

Synthetic - Round

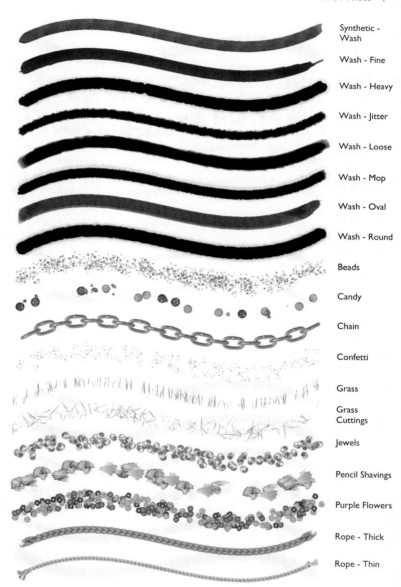

Synthetic - Wash

Wash - Fine

Wash - Heavy

Wash - Jitter

Wash - Loose

Wash - Mop

Wash - Oval

Wash - Round

Beads

Candy

Chain

Confetti

Grass

Grass Cuttings

Jewels

Pencil Shavings

Purple Flowers

Rope - Thick

Rope - Thin

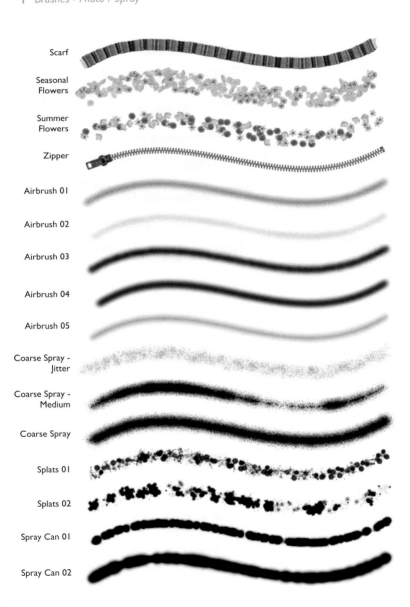

Scarf

Seasonal
Flowers

Summer
Flowers

Zipper

Airbrush 01

Airbrush 02

Airbrush 03

Airbrush 04

Airbrush 05

Coarse Spray -
Jitter

Coarse Spray -
Medium

Coarse Spray

Splats 01

Splats 02

Spray Can 01

Spray Can 02

Design Templates

This chapter provides a reference gallery of the design templates included with DrawPlus X4.

The design templates can be accessed from the Startup Wizard and include **Arts & Crafts**, **Education**, **Logos**, **Posters**, **Web Banners**, and **Greeting Cards** categories. Be sure to check out the keyframe animation design templates in the **Animated Web Banners** category!

The **Arts & Crafts** category includes **Pop-up Cards**, **Colouring-In**, **Cootie Catchers**, **Paper Crafts**, **Scrapbooking**, and **Wrapping Paper**. All of these templates are interactive and ready for you to print out and use.

Where necessary, we have provided illustrations of how the templates will look when printed out, cut out, and folded.

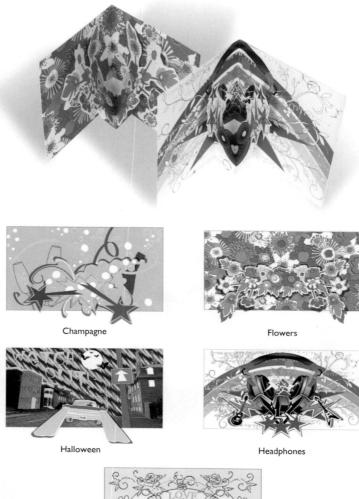

Champagne

Flowers

Halloween

Headphones

True Love

Space Aliens

Farmer

Ice Cream

Pirates

Cootie Catchers

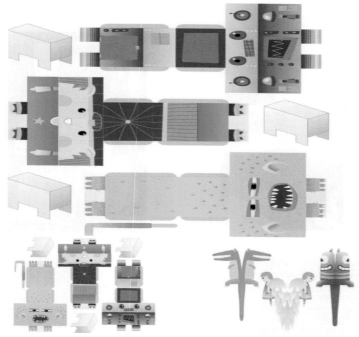

Box Toys

Cocktail Characters

Space Toy

Nursery Mobiles

Shuttle

Jet Plane

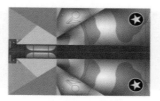

Camping

Messy Desk

Blue Stripes

Flowers

Hearts

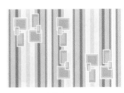

Ice Cream

Kids

Modern

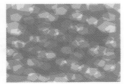

Petals

Pink Crackle

Space

Periodic Table

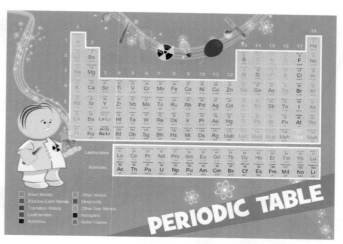

Alphabet Chart

Balanced Diet

School Play.

Secondary School Class Timetable

African Art Show

Book Store

Classic Car Show

Coffee Morning

Country Folk

Dance Event

Flower Show

Folk Festival

Garden Festival

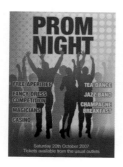

Prom Night

Record Fair

Record Sale

Village Fair

Butterfly Menu

Cafe Now Open

Dancing Club

Drinks Offers

Italian Restaurant

Lounge Club

Party Club

Restaurant Open Soon

Action Movie

Car Sales

City At Night Movie

Education Crafts

Environment Notice

Looking For Love Movie

Performance Management

Sci-Fi Movie

Closing Down

Cruise Offer

Discount Swirly

Dressmakers

Everything Dropped

Fine Wines

Flower Bouquet

Fresh Skin Care

Music Shop

New Year Sale

Open Day

Organic Cosmetics

Shirts Spring Deals

Splash Out

Spring Sale Motif

Store Banner

Summer Collection

Sunglasses Offer

The Fruit Tree

Tropical Holidays

Urban Alternative Retail

Web Banners

The DrawPlus **Design Templates** include **Animated Web Banners** and **Static Web Banners** sections.

Both animated and static web banners are easy to insert into and edit on your own web pages.

Web Banners - Animated

Animated web banners are **keyframe animation** documents. The example below illustrates various stages of the animation—why not open one and preview it for yourself?

Chocoholics

College

Green Solutions

Holiday Adventures

Outdoors

Red City

Regina

Restaurant

Tricore

Chocoholics College Epoc Solutions Digital Media

Outdoors Restaurant Web Hosting

Web Banners - Static

Animals

Casino

Digital Camera

Digital Media

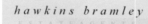

Estate Agents

Green Solutions

Health & Beauty

Lunar Eclipse

Martial Arts

Music

Orange Orb

Tricore

Web Hosting

Wine

xytron

Animals

Casino

Digital Camera

Digital Media

Estate Agents

Green Solutions

Health & Beauty

Lunar Eclipse

Luxury Hotel

Martial Arts

Music

Orange Orb

Tricore

Web Hosting

Wine

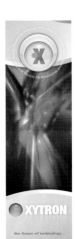

xytron

Animals

Bees

Dinosaur

Elephants

Footballer

Frog

Gardener

Guitar

Motorbike

Party

Rugby

Sunflower

Tennis

Trees

Bauble

Christmas Cheer

Christmas Pud

Christmas Puddings

Mistletoe

Nativity

Robin

Santa

Snowflakes

Snowman

Abstract Canvas

Baby Boy

Baby Girl

Ballerina Thanks

Be My Valentine

Champagne

Circles

Congratulations
Wedding Cake

Cute Hearts

Easter Egg

First Day at
School

Get Well Soon
Teddy

Graduation

Halloween

I Love You

I'm Sorry

Just Married

Leaving Rooster

Mothers Day

New Arrival
Bunnies

Passed Driving
Test

Relax

Retirement

Sorry

Thank You

Samples

To demonstrate the incredible flexibility of DrawPlus, we've provided you with a varied collection of sample documents.

The samples include stunning soft pencil lines created with the graphic soft shading brushes, impressive effects created with the new blend modes, and a varied selection of posters and animations.

We hope they'll inspire you to create your own works of art!

'Cherry Blossom' sample created using the **Erase** and **Multiply** blend modes.

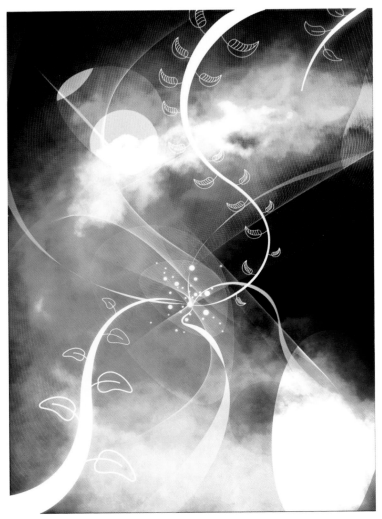

'Vision' sample created using the **Colour Burn** and **Overlay** blend modes.

'Graphic Soft Pencil' sample created with the **Graphic Soft Shading** brushes.

'Manga' sample created using pressure sensitivity and a graphics tablet.

Chalk Tree

Karate Dan

Teddy Bear

Fireball

Charcoal Elephant

Watercolour Sunrise

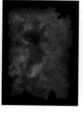

Grunge Brushes

Pastel Still Life

Watercolour
Flowers

Cloudy Night

Watercolour Tree

Pears

Dancing Club

Space Aliens

Dressmakers

Ice Cream

Party Club

Pirates

Jigsaw (interactive)

Village Fair

Alien Alone

Bruiser George

Come Back Soon

Concert Poster

Floral Escape

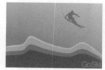

Go Ski

Little Devil Billy

Mum Son and Dog

Sports Car

Office Daydream

Portrait

Robot Convention
2020

Space Boys

Space Child

The Tree of
Forgotten Guilt

Watercolour

Pastel City

Bird on a Rock

Bridge

Dog

Electricity

Fishing

Still Life

Toucan

World Window

Bass Synth

Bike

Drinks On Us

Electric Fan

Golf

Radio Days

Shark

Technical

Watch

Scooter

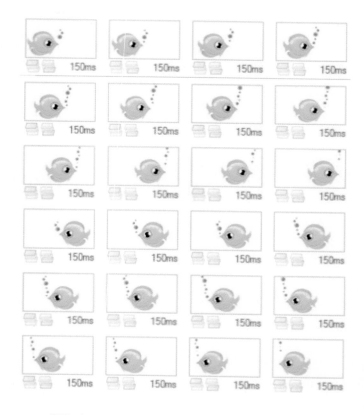

'Fish' animation sample, showing the frames on the **Storyboard** tab.

Cat Running
(animated)

Lamp (animated)

Watch (animated)